GOD OUR FATHER

The Only True God

WRITTEN BY
RYAN COMER

Table of Contents

Introduction
1 Foundation 1
2 God as a Father 4
3 One or Only God Being the Father 7
4 God Is Our and Jesus's Father 18
5 Jesus Teaches How to Pray 86
6 Jesus Was Raised by God 91
7 Jesus Given Authority by God 121
8 Through or in Jesus 147
9 Jesus is a Man 175
10 Jesus Belongs to God 186
11 Jesus is With God, Not is God 189
12 Revelation 195
Conclusion 203
Scripture Index 207

Introduction

There has been for centuries a heated debate (at times resulting in death) which has great significance in relation to eternal life between those who profess Jesus to be the Messiah of Israel, and savior of the world. The subject of the debate, does God consist of multiple yet distinct persons, providing a great "mystery", or is He very simply, the Father, alone.

The Almighty has told us about scripture that *"The secret things belong to the Lord our God, but the things that are revealed belong to us and to our children forever"*[1]. So, I believe the answer is quite simple according to scripture and is not a mystery we are to accept by faith. I do not see the need for a council or church confession to explain something that is so obvious to the objective and observant eye.

Thus, with confidence I can say, I have discovered the conclusion of this issue is not in agreement with the Orthodox doctrine held by the church for over sixteen hundred years. It is rather contrary and makes those who espouse this say the very messiah that was sent to save us, and his apostles were believers and teachers of idolatry. How so? They did this by supposedly exalting Jesus to be their God as well.

---

[1] Deuteronomy 29:29

As I go through the text, I have chosen to use *Jesus* in my references to the Messiah so there will be no confusion as to who I am referring to.

I want the reader to understand. This is not a debate. I do not plan to attempt addressing the common debated passages, for that is not my purpose or desire. I only wish to lay a different starting point for building one's "theology" of who God is. In doing this I hope to stir the reader to put aside what has always been held as truth and not seek to refute the evidence laid out in this book, but instead, take the time necessary to read the information and search the scriptures themselves.

In compiling this work I have spent a considerable amount of time to present the facts I have found. And, as I continue in my study in scripture, I am sure there will be much more I can add to this work. Thus, it is not exhaustive, or at least not as in-depth as I am sure it can be.

In preparing for the opening chapter, I leave this quote to consider, *"The scriptures," it is said," reveal many things as facts which they do not undertake to explain." As an example, the declaration "God is a Spirit "is cited. Now we demand the similar declaration announcing the fact that God is a triune being. A fact is not a matter of mere inference from something which is said; it must be declared in so many words or be shown to be necessarily implied in something else which is stated as a fact"*[2].

I pray this is a benefit to all who read it and that the Creator will bless this work for His glory.

Shalom, Ryan Comer

---

[2] *Unitarian Advocate, Vol. 1*, 1828, Rev. Edmund Q. Sewell

1 Foundation

Before going any further, I want to be sure it is understood, as most agree, YHWH[3] is clearly said to be one being. This is one of the major doctrines that sets those who believe in the Bible, both Jews and Christians, apart from all other religions. The Shema, as it is titled, from Deuteronomy[4], lays this foundation for us when it says, *"Hear O' Israel, YHWH your God, YHWH is one"*. A Jewish friend I have had contact with gave me a more proper understanding of this saying "The interpretation of the Shema has changed in modern times to reflect a defensive position against the Trinity by stating God is one. But Trinitarians have reinterpreted that to mean "one compound". However, the traditional and more sensible interpretation has been "Hear O Israel, YHWH is our God, YHWH alone." It is already presumed that there is only one YHWH and that He is not a corporate being"[5].

---

[3] This is the name of the God of scripture and is called by many the Tetragrammaton which consist of the Hebrew letters, Yod Hey Vav Hey. Most believe the name should be pronounced as Yahweh, which from my research shows to be true. This is not certain though.

[4] Deuteronomy 6:4

[5] Yeremyah Natzraya

With that being said, any person who accepts that the Bible is God's word must also accept there is only one God and not many.

As this is the basis for the theology of who and what God is, the exposition of the "New Testament" must agree with this fact. Due to this fact, most honest scholars and teachers would agree, the Tanakh[6] does not reveal a multi-person God, especially if one were to read it alone.

Therefore, without the New Testament, which the majority of those who keep to a multi-person God say is "the Old Testament revealed", it is very doubtful that there would be such a concept of a multi-person God amongst those who proclaim to receive scripture as truth.

There is one thing that is certain concerning the personhood of the Almighty. The Old Testament[7] irrefutably reveals a singular being who speaks or is identified as a *He, Him, I, Me,* etc...[8] and not a multi-personal being.

---

[6] The Jews call the Old Testament the Tanakh, which "is an acronym that identifies the Hebrew Bible. The acronym is based on the initial Hebrew letters of each of the text's three parts: 1. Torah [תורה] meaning one or all of: "The Law"; "Teaching"; "Instruction". Also called the *Chumash* [חמש] meaning: "The five"; "The five books of Moses". It is the "Pentateuch". 2. Nevi'im [נביאים] meaning: "Prophets" 3. Ketuvim [כתובים] meaning "Writings" www.bibliahebraica.com

[7] This holds true for the New Testament as well

[8] This is attested to 11,000 times in the Old Testament alone

With all of this considered, it is essential for those seeking to prove a multi-person God, that they use the New Testament writers' concept of who God is as evidence for defending that this being consists of more than one person[9]. Due to these circumstances, I will focus on the New Testament writings.

Before I delve any further into this topic, I want to leave the reader with this thought to consider as they read through this book. Can it rationally and linguistically be shown that more than one person can speak as a singular being as is claimed?

---

[9] The New Testament supposedly explains "clearly" that God is three, or as some say, two persons. This is not supported at all by a non-debatable statement stating such, which alone should cause questions to be asked

2 God as a Father

I think it necessary to begin by establishing that the belief of God being spoken of as our Father is not a New Testament phenomenon. It is prominently written in the Old Testament (which was the source that Jesus built all his teaching on). Here are a handful of such texts:

- *"You must say to Pharaoh, 'Thus says the LORD, "Israel is my son, my firstborn" (Exodus 4:22),*
- *"And I said to you, 'Let my son go that he may serve me,' but since you have refused to let him go, I will surely kill your son, your firstborn" (Exodus 4:23),*
- *"I will become his father and he will become my son. When he sins, I will correct him with the rod of men and with wounds inflicted by human beings" (2 Samuel 7:14),*
- *"He is a father to the fatherless and an advocate for widows. God rules from his holy palace" (Psalm 68:5),*
- *"As a father has compassion on his children, so the LORD has compassion on his faithful followers (Psalm 103:13),*

- *"For the LORD disciplines those he loves, just as a father disciplines the son in whom he delights" (Proverbs 3:12),*
- *"For you are our Father, though Abraham does not know us, and Israel does not acknowledge us; you, O LORD, are our Father, our Redeemer from of old is your name" (Isaiah 63:16),*
- *"Yet, LORD, you are our father. We are the clay, and you are our potter; we are all the product of your labor" (Isaiah 64:8),*
- *"I said, how I would set you among my sons, and give you a pleasant land, a heritage most beautiful of all nations. And I thought you would call me, My Father, and would not turn from following me" (Jeremiah 3:19),*
- *"With weeping they shall come, and with pleas for mercy I will lead them back, I will make them walk by brooks of water, in a straight path in which they shall not stumble, for I am a father to Israel, and Ephraim is my firstborn" (Jeremiah 31:9),*
- *"A son naturally honors his father and a slave respects his master. If I am your father, where is my honor? If I am your master, where is my respect? The LORD who rules over all asks you this, you priests who make light of my name! But you reply, 'How have we made light of your name" (Malachi 1:6),*
- *"Do we not all have one father? Did not one God create us? Why do we betray one another, in this*

way making light of the covenant of our ancestors" (Malachi 2:10)

So, it can without question be seen that YHWH is the only God, and that He is the Father of every man, especially Israel.

With this as the starting point in understanding the personhood of God, I shall continue to present from the New Testament evidence that will convincingly reveal that this being that the New Testament calls our Father is by Himself the YHWH of Israel.

3 One or Only God Being the Father

That *only* or *one* are attached to the Father when He is addressed as God, I believe, demands that God consists of one person alone. Now, as we ensue to determine the truthfulness of the preceding statement, this fact must be taken into consideration; the most prominent way God speaks to man is through our language. In doing so, He allows us to intelligibly understand what He desires us to know through using our ability to make reasonable conclusions from the information He has given us.

With this in mind, let's apply this to a passage in John's gospel. John says *"this is eternal life, to know you, the only true God, and Jesus Christ, whom you sent"*[10]. In this prayer it must be remembered that Jesus is speaking to the Father, as the beginning of the prayer shows.[11] Therefore, by using *only*, Jesus is telling us there is no one who is truly God but the Father.[12]

---

[10] John 17:3

[11] His statement *"Father, the hour has come"* shows the words *"only true God"* are directed toward the Father

[12] This is a major linguistic mountain needing to be climbed. As far as I am aware the *only* does not allow the remotest possibility of any other entity to be included with what is the *only*

The Rotherham Emphasized Bible, which is a hyper literal translation, reads this way, *"and this, is the age–abiding life, that they get to know thee, the only real God, and him whom thou didst send, Jesus Christ"*. The Greek word translated as *only* in this verse is *monos*. Thayer's Lexicon[13] gives these definitions: *alone (without a companion), forsaken, destitute of help, alone, only, merely*. Considering these possible uses of *monos*, *alone* seems to me the most appropriate.

What makes this so important is that the word *God* is only applicable to the one said to be such. Thus, the Father, who Jesus is referring to, is solely God.

The gospel also records these words spoken by Jesus, *"I have come in my Father's name, and you do not receive me. If another comes in his own name, you will receive him. How can you believe, when you receive glory from one another and do not seek the glory that comes from the only God."*[14] Here once again we find *only God* being connected to the Father. This coincides perfectly with the verse previously quoted.

I also want to address a couple of other things related to this passage that are important to consider,

---

[13] *A Greek-English Lexicon of the New Testament,* Joseph Henry Thayer; New York: Harper & Brothers 1889

[14] John 5:43-44

that being; what is his Father's name and how does it relate to Jesus?

When looking at the messiah's Hebrew[15] name, how he could say he came in his Father's name can be seen clearly by his own testimony. Jesus says about this *"...Holy Father, keep them in your name, which you have given me, that they may be one, even as we are one"*. In this we find he was named by the Almighty Himself, something which is extremely significant. A description of this is found in the gospel of Matthew,[16] which tells us what the angel instructed Joseph to name the child, that being *Yahshua* or *Yeshua*.[17]

There is contained within the name given to this child a picture of what he was sent to do. It is defined as Y*HWH saves*. This makes perfect sense because as Matthew records *"he will save his people from their sins"*[18].

In Luke's gospel he gives the account of Mary also being given a message from an angel concerning

---

[15] Some suggest Aramaic was the source of his name. But many other scholars reject that and acknowledge Hebrew to be its origin of which I agree with. The reason being that the Greek word *Εβραΐς* (pronounced *Hebrais*) is transliterated as *Hebrew* and not *Aramaic*

[16] The concept of the virgin birth found in both Matthew and Luke, has for some time been questioned as to its authenticity. Though I agree that it is an addition to the original writer, I have used it due to the fact that it is not seen as such by those who hold to a multi-person God

[17] This is debated though most scholars agree it is *Yeshua*

[18] Matthew 1:21, Luke 1:31

this child to be born, that being he *"will be great and will be called the Son of the Most-High. And the Lord God will give to him the throne of his father David"*[19].

Looking at this evidence it should be clear how Jesus could say that he came in *his Father's name* and why this name was given to him. Furthermore, it confirms the fact that when Jesus says, *"the only God"*, he is referring to the Father.

First Corinthians chapter eight verse six is another witness that confirms this truth[20]. It reads *"Yet for us there is one God, the Father..."*. The context of this verse is explaining that there is only one who is truly God[21], as is clarified in verse four *"therefore, as to the eating of food offered to idols, we know that "an idol has no real existence," and that "there is no God but one"*.

Along with this, another significant thing to bring our attention to is the use of the conjunction *and*. With this little word the Apostle divides *one God* (the Father) from *one lord* (Jesus). The fact that God is used in connection with the Father, and not the second party mentioned, makes it impossible for anyone other than Him to be God.

On an aside, pertaining to the second half of verse six, I have heard these words, *"one Lord, Jesus*

---

[19] Luke 1:32
[20] This passage also helps solidify that "only God" can be attached to none other than the Father
[21] which is what Jesus declared in John 17:3

Christ, through whom are all things and through whom we live[22]", used as evidence that Jesus is God (LORD). But the use of Lord (*kurios*) being applied to Jesus in this instance can in no way suggest him to be God, seeing we find in another place the Apostles say, *God has made him both <u>Lord</u> and Christ.*[23]

Thus, according to the apostle, there is no God but one, and for us this one God is affirmed to be the Father. Hence, though there are many so called gods worshipped by the world, the one and only God for us is the Father, not a triune or biune being.

Continuing on with Paul's letters, he tells his readers in Ephesus *"There is one body and one Spirit, just as you too were called to the one hope of your calling, one Lord, one faith, one baptism, one God and Father of all, who is over all and through all and in all"*.[24] In this passage there is something very similar to what is seen in the first Corinthians text, that being, there is...*one lord <u>and</u> one God and Father.*[25] Here though, the apostle goes into even more detail saying this God is *"the Father of all who is over all and through all and in all"*. *This is* akin to a statement from chapter eight verse six of first Corinthians that reads *"from whom are all things and for whom we live"*. This particular description is later

---

[22] I will not address the words *"through whom are all things and through whom we live"*, for as I have said, I do not intend to debate
[23] Acts 2:36
[24] Ephesians 4:4-6
[25] as Malachi 2:10 declares

given in first Corinthians to the one who put all things under the Messiahs feet. It reads, *"when all things are subjected to him, then the Son himself will also be subjected to him who put all things in subjection under him that God may be all in all".*[26]

In reading this passage about all things being subjected to the son, you can go to Luke chapter one verse thirty-one and see this same idea detailed by the angel. We find that the son is in a place of authority because it is given to him by the Father. He writes *"the Lord God will give to him the throne of his father David".*[27] But there will come the time when he *delivereth up the kingdom unto his God and Father."*[28]

Therefore, When the Fathers plan is accomplished and all of his enemies are put under the feet of the Messiah, He will be all in all and reign without a representative as King over His people as the scripture declares, *"The dwelling place of God is with man. He will dwell with them, and they will be his people, and God himself will be with them as their God".*[29]

---

[26] 1 Corinthians 15:28

[27] Interestingly, the throne of David is also called the throne of God *"Then Solomon sat on the throne of the Lord as king in place of David his father". 1 Chronicles 29:23*

[28] 1Corinthians 15:24 *Rotherham Emphasized Bible*

[29] Revelation 21:3

Furthermore, in this Ephesians text there is an obvious distinction between each subject mentioned, that is, there is one of each; body, spirit, hope, baptism, and ending with one *God and Father*. And to make it even more evident that there is but one person who God consists of, the text says *of all, who is over all*. This will be addressed later in showing Jesus himself has a God.

Next, we find in the letter of first Timothy another text illustrating who God is[30] according to the New Testament writers. It says, *"There is one God, and there is one mediator between God and men, the man Christ Jesus"*.[31] Though this verse does not overtly describe this one God as being the Father, it can definitely be verified to be so from the beginning of the epistle which says, *"Paul, an apostle of Jesus Christ by the commandment of God our Savior, and Lord Jesus Christ, which is our hope; Grace, mercy, and peace from God our Father and Christ Jesus our Lord"*.[32] Furthermore, he follows a few verses later with *"now to the King eternal, immortal, invisible, the only wise God, be honor and glory for ever and ever. Amen"*.[33] These two texts show exactly what person the one God in chapter two verse five is speaking of. This greeting in first Timothy says of this that; God is our savior, Paul became an apostle by His command, and He is our Father. Along with

---

[30] Which Jesus said was necessary for eternal life
[31] 1 Timothy 2:5
[32] 1 Timothy 1:1-2 *King James Version*
[33] 1 Timothy 1:17 *King James Version*

this he writes in verse seventeen in this chapter that the *King eternal* is the *only wise God*. We do find Jesus referred to twice within in these verses, but never is he described as being God. Furthermore, in chapter two it can be seen the word *mediator* is independent from the title *God* due to the conjunction *and* being used once more, just as it is with the phrase *between God and man*, which explicitly shows there is one who is God and there is one who is mediator. What's more, the letter shows Jesus isn't just separated from the person of God by the term *and*. He is also called a *man* who mediates between man and God. Being he is a man who mediates between God and man, the logical conclusion is he is neither of those he is between. He is not God, nor is he the men he mediates for. Thus, the text clearly tells us God is our savior, Father, the only wise God who is the king eternal, immortal, invisible and He is the one God. Whereas concerning Jesus, he is said to be our hope, our lord[34] and our mediator.

That said, Paul doesn't seem to have any idea of a multi-person, one being God, as he is accused of by most Christians, or at least to this point.

In James' letter he proclaims as well that there is only one God saying, *"you believe that there is one God: you do well..."*[35] But how can the reader be confident that he is referring only to the Father? Just

---

[34] Lord when connected to Jesus never suggests he is LORD as Acts 2:36 makes clear
[35] James 2:19

as the other writers of the New Testament, his greeting presents clear evidence which reads, *"James, a servant of God <u>and</u> of the Lord Jesus Christ*[36] along with *Every good gift and every perfect gift is from above, and comes down from the Father of lights, with whom is no fickleness, neither shadow of turning".*[37] Another thing that reinforces this to be accurate is found in Acts; *"They lifted their voices together to God and said, "Sovereign Lord, who made the heaven and the earth and the sea and everything in them, who through the mouth of our father David, your servant, said by the Holy Spirit, "'Why did the Gentiles rage, and the peoples plot in vain? The kings of the earth set them-selves, and the rulers were gathered together, against the Lord and against his Anointed'- for truly in this city there were gathered together against your holy servant Jesus, whom you anointed, both Herod and Pontius Pilate, along with the Gentiles and the peoples of Israel, to do whatever your hand and your plan had predestined to take place. And now, Lord, look upon their threats and grant to your servants to continue to speak your word with all boldness, while you stretch out your hand to heal, and signs and wonders are performed through the name of your holy servant Jesus".*[38] In this prayer prompted by persecution, James was without a doubt present, being he was an elder of the church in Jerusalem as chapter fifteen

---

[36] James 1:1
[37] James 1:17
[38] Acts 4:24-30

con-firms. In this prayer the writer states that Jesus was anointed as the holy servant *of* the LORD. This God who anointed him is said by the disciples to be the *"Sovereign Lord, who made the heaven and the earth and the sea and everything in them."* We find that Jesus himself concurs with this saying *"I thank you, Father, Lord of heaven and earth."*[39]

Another interesting thing to note is the mention of God speaking through David. I say this because of what the writer of Hebrews tells us, that being, *but in these last days he has spoken to us by his Son.* This gives a clear example of the Father speaking through His Son, the prophet spoken of to come, just as He did through the prophets of old.[40]

Taking all of this into account, James (as well as Jesus) undoubtedly believed what every other writer did, the one God of scripture consists of the Father alone.

In another letter, that of Jude[41], he is also in agreement with James[42] saying, *"Now to him who is able to keep you from stumbling and to present you*

---

[39] Matthew 11:25, Luke 10:21

[40] You can also see Jesus say such in abundance in John's Gospel

[41] Many say this writer is the brother of Jesus, as they do with James. So, I, seeing there is little evidence to completely reject this, have used this relationship to make a stronger point

[42] Both Jude and James are said to be brothers of Jesus, which is seen in Luke 8:20 and Mark 3:32 which say, "And a crowd was sitting around him, and they said to him, "Your mother and your brothers are outside, seeking you." This is an odd statement if they knew, especially his mother, that he was their God as well

blameless before the presence of his glory with great joy, to the only God, our Savior, through Jesus Christ our Lord, be glory, majesty, dominion, and authority, before all time and now and forever. Amen".[43] So, we have the writer here saying that glory, majesty, dominion and authority are all to be seen through Jesus and belong to the only God, who is someone other than the Messiah.

If it is accepted that these two are brothers of Jesus, I would consider their words to be quite authoritative and particularly weighty when defining who they understood their brother to be, as well as his relationship with their God.

These texts are undeniable proof that the person unchangingly referred to as this one God, is the Father and no one else. There can be no other conclusion if indeed one is willing to be "cast out of the synagogue" for the truth. It is my hopes that is who this finds.

---

[43] Jude 1:25

4 God Is Our and Jesus's Father

There is another fact that must be acknowledged by the student of scripture, that being, that God is repeatedly designated as the Father of Jesus. With this in mind, I will further exhibit through a wealth of texts that the Father alone is God.

Before I get to the scripture, I would like to point out once more the significance of the word *and* to amplify its importance in understanding the personhood of God. The reason being, that this word is used nearly every time the term God and Jesus/Christ are mentioned together.

It is especially critical as well to note that the labels *son* or *son of* are used in relation to Jesus one hundred and eighty-eight times in the New Testament. Whereas God is depicted as *Father* or *Father of* two hundred and fifty-eight times in the New Testament. Never is God used in conjunction with Jesus.[44] I find it extremely puzzling how, for the sake of preserving a doctrine, this fact seems to be glossed over as insignificant by those clinging to an illogical mythical mystery.

---

[44] There are a handful of verses that are used to suggest otherwise, though their grammar and authenticity are questionable (Acts 20:28, Titus 2:13, 2 Peter 1:1)

In presenting the texts showing God to be our Father and the Father of Jesus, I will also give some commentary to clarify this fact.

1. Jesus said to her, "Do not cling to me, for I have not yet ascended to the Father; but go to my brothers and say to them, 'I am ascending to my Father and your Father, to my God and your God. Mary Magdalene went and announced to the disciples, "I have seen the Lord"-and that he had said these things to her—John 20:17-18

One of the most exalted proof texts for the "multi-person God" is found in this very same chapter. Sadly though, the horrendous use of this one verse undermines the context of the entire chapter it is contained in by reason of the contention just mentioned. If we are to accept this, it would have to be concluded that verses seventeen and eighteen are deceptive and do not mean what they say. Though there is deception involved, the chicanery is not in the words spoken by Jesus, nor those of Thomas, but rather the interpretation of them.

So, in conflict to my purpose for writing this book and to confirm that Thomas's proclamation is misinterpreted, I want to shift from the subject of this chapter to look at the entire event leading up to when these words are spoken by the disciple.

Beginning in verse seventeen we are told that Jesus had appeared to Mary[45] who was then given a

---

[45] It is interesting how Mary addressed Jesus when she saw him in

message to relay to the disciples beginning with him saying *"go tell my brothers"*.⁴⁶ This she does as she tells them *he had said these things to her*.⁴⁷ So what was it she was commanded to tell those whom Jesus called *brothers*? He states, that I am *"ascending to my Father and your Father, to my God and your God"*.

Considering Jesus spoke these words, it is evident he did not identify himself to be their God, but rather their brother who had the same Father and God. Following this incident, he appears to the other disciples as well, though apparently it was with the exception of Thomas.

When Jesus manifested himself to them, he says, *"peace be with you. As the Father has sent me, even so I am sending you"*⁴⁸ Notice that he says *the Father has sent me* and not *my Father*. This is especially important since it reveals God is not just his Father but the Father of all, as I previously showed from Malachi, *"have we not all one Father? Has not one God created us?..."*⁴⁹ Later when Thomas is present *"the other disciples told him, "We have seen the*

---

verse sixteen, that being *"She turned and said to him in Aramaic, "Rabboni!" (which means Teacher)."* This is quite a different response to that of Thomas, which I think is very noteworthy

⁴⁶ This is a most ridiculous command if indeed he were to be God, for God has no brother. It also appears Mary was not shocked by him making such a statement, suggesting she has no idea of his divinity

⁴⁷ It must be remembered this is said by Jesus after his resurrection

⁴⁸ John 20:21.

⁴⁹ Malachi 2:10

*Lord"*⁵⁰, which Thomas would not believe unless he saw him with his own eyes. This shows the context in which Thomas declares my *Lord and my God*. Thus, I find it very strange that Jesus would have Mary tell his *brothers*, with Thomas being included, that he was ascending to *"my Father and your Father, to my God and your God"*, yet Thomas for some unknown reason tells the messiah he is also his God.

Exactly what Thomas meant by this or if he was even saying this about Jesus, I will not address as I stated in the opening.⁵¹ But I do know that within the framework of this chapter, that claim has no basis whatsoever that agrees with the claims concerning what Thomas meant by those words. It is, on the other hand, unmistakable that Jesus declares *my Father…my God,* which needs no interpretation concerning his meaning in saying such. This clarifies to us that when Jesus called God his Father, he is telling us there is no God but the Father.

2. *In that same hour he rejoiced in the Holy Spirit and said, "I thank you, Father, Lord of heaven and earth, that you have hidden these things from the wise and understanding and revealed them to little child-ren; yes, Father, for such was your gracious will.—Luke 10:21*

---

⁵⁰ John 20:25

⁵¹ Something else intriguing is the fact that Thomas did not make the statement until he touched Jesus. Does that somehow suggest he was God, because he was confirmed to be raised from the dead?

Jesus, as I mentioned previously, here states the Father to be Lord of heaven and earth. As I also mentioned in relationship with this, his disciples also declared this in Acts, *"when they heard it, they lifted their voices together to God and said, "Sovereign Lord, who made the heaven and the earth and the sea and every-thing in them, who through the mouth of our father David, your servant, said by the Holy Spirit, "'Why did the Gentiles rage, and the peoples plot in vain? The kings of the earth set themselves, and the rulers were gathered together, against the Lord and against his Anointed'- for truly in this city there were gathered together against your holy servant Jesus, whom you anointed, both Herod and Pontius Pilate, along with the Gentiles and the peoples of Israel, to do whatever your hand and your plan had predestined to take place. And now, Lord, look upon their threats and grant to your servants to continue to speak your word with all boldness, while you stretch out your hand to heal, and signs and wonders are performed through the name of your holy servant Jesus"*.[52] Both Jesus, his disciples, and obviously the Old Testament, declare God Almighty made the heavens and the earth, of which there is no debate.[53] What does cause dispute, is the claim that Jesus is also this Lord of heaven and earth. The facts though refute this erroneous claim. Reason one: he

---

[52] Acts 4:24-30

[53] . I would also like to point out that scripture says *"...A matter may be legally established only on the testimony of two or three witnesses"-Deuteronomy 19:15*

himself says the Father is; and reason two: Jesus is termed *"your holy servant"* by his followers in Acts, with *your* referring to the Sovereign Lord, who the writer explains, anointed him.

Something else in the verse being examined in Luke's Gospel are his statements, *"that you have hidden these things from the wise and understanding"* and *"for such was your gracious will"*. If we consider that this is connected to the one he says is Lord of heaven and earth, the logical conclusion would be that this Lord of heaven and earth is such alone.

Within the scripture from Acts there is one last thing to draw attention to, that being God allowed the persons mentioned *"to do whatever (His) hand and (His) plan had predestined* which most certainly fits into the Fathers *gracious will* spoken of in Luke. The person that had been predestined is His *holy servant*, Jesus, who in another place said *My Father, if it be possible, let this cup pass from me; nevertheless, not as I will, but as you will"*.[54]

The question must be asked, will we heed the Almighty who said, *"this is my beloved Son;* **listen to him***"?*[55]

3. *Paul, a servant of Jesus Christ, called to be an apostle, separated to the gospel of God, (Which He had promised before by His prophets in the holy*

---

[54] Matthew 26:39b
[55] Mark 9:7

scriptures,)Concerning His Son Jesus Christ our Lord, which was made of the seed of David according to the flesh; And declared to be the Son of God with power, according to the spirit of holiness, by the resurrection from the dead: By whom we have received grace and apostleship, for obedience to the faith among all nations, for his name: Among whom are you also the called of Jesus Christ: To all that be in Rome, beloved of God, called to be saints: Grace to you and peace from God our Father, and the Lord Jesus Christ. First, I thank my God through Jesus Christ for you all, that your faith is spoken of throughout the whole world. For God is my witness, whom I serve with my spirit in the gospel of His Son, that without ceasing I make mention of you always in my – Romans 1:1-10

There are numerous illuminating details in this passage that help in having a more secure knowledge on this subject. The first thing to draw attention to is the words "*gospel of God*" which are connected to "*He had promised...concerning His son*". The statement *gospel of God* is also seen in first Timothy chapter one verse eleven, "*according to the glorious gospel of the blessed God, which was committed to my trust*". Take notice of the word *He* and *His* within these ten verses of Romans. In order, the first mention says *He promised*; second, *His prophets*; and third, *His son*.[56] The statement *gospel of God*

---

[56] This wording *His son* is said twice of Jesus with *His* referring to God

tells us who *He* and *His* are referring to, that obviously being God. Seeing that God is the one these pronouns are applied to; it must stand then that the things which are described as be-longing to Him cannot be God. Moreover, seeing that the gospel was concerning His son, the reasonable conclusion is that *He* is speaking of the Father being this God, seeing a son must have a father.

To further define who the *He/His* of this passage is, I want to examine the uses of the title *God*. This word is found four times, and not once is it shared with or joined to Jesus/the son, which logically eliminates him to be considered as a participant it can be applied to. That leaves only one other choice, the Father, with the defining statement being *"God our Father"*. Here are clear descriptions of who the word *God* is being applied to, which are:

- Gospel of God (the Father) … concerning His son
- Peace from God our Father
- I thank my God (the Father) through Jesus Christ
- God is my witness whom I serve in… the gospel of His (the Father) son.

There is one thing the apostle clearly does reveal about Jesus though, he is God's son, which Paul writes three times. This is a clear doctrine concerning him.

4. Now the God of patience and consolation grant you to be like minded one toward another according to Christ Jesus: That you may with one mind and one mouth glorify the God and Father of our Lord Jesus Christ. Receive you one another, as Christ also received us to the glory of God. — Romans 15:5-7

These verses are written in the same letter as the previously cited verses, and within them is one of the clearest examples pertaining to the subject at hand regarding the person of God, that being, *"the God and Father of our Lord Jesus Christ"*.

In the opening of these verses the apostle writes *"the God of patience and consolation grant you to be like minded"* with the result being that the believers glorify God *with one mind and one mouth*. As has been mentioned he tells us the one being glorified is *"the God and Father of our lord Jesus"*. This leads to the conclusion that when *God* is used here, or throughout this epistle, it can only be referring to Jesus's God and Father.

As well, it should be noted that God is seen three times in these verses and is never linked with anyone other than the Father. I would hope the very fact that Paul writes *"God and Father of"* is sufficient to reveal to the reader who he understood to be God.

In ending, we are told to receive each other as Christ received us with the end result being *"to the glory of God"*. So, it would lead from the context that it would mean *"to the glory of the God and Father of* *our Lord Jesus", * just as it would undoubtedly have to every time the apostle speaks of God.

5. *Paul called to be an apostle of Jesus Christ through the will of God, and Sosthenes our brother, To the church of God which is at Corinth, to them that are sanctified in Christ Jesus, called to be saints, with all that in every place call on the name of Jesus Christ our Lord, both theirs and ours: Grace be to you, and peace, from God our Father, and from the Lord Jesus Christ. I thank my God always on your behalf, for the grace of God which is given you in Jesus Christ; That in everything you are enriched by Him, in all utterance, and in all knowledge; Even as the testimony of Christ was confirmed in you: So that you come behind in no gift; waiting for the coming of our Lord Jesus Christ: Who shall also confirm you to the end, that you may be blameless in the day of our Lord Jesus Christ. God is faithful, by whom you were called to the fellowship of His Son Jesus Christ our Lord.—1Corinthians 1:1-9*

Something to note before continuing. Second Corinthians, Ephesians, Colossians, and Second Timothy all say in the first verse of the letter the very same thing Paul writes here, *"called to be an apostle of Jesus Christ through*[57] *the will of God"*. Paul makes clear in every letter he writes that he is *an apostle of Jesus Christ,* not because he or a man

---

[57] The Greek word **διά** *(dia)* translated here as *through* is also translated as *by* in many places which causes problems in certain places where something is *dia* Jesus

chose it to be so, but rather, *"through the will of God"*. Be aware that the will of God is never spoken of as the will of Jesus. Instead, as our messiah taught us to pray *"our Father...your will be done" (Matthew 6:9a, 10b)*.

Another thing in common with each of these epistles is the phrase *"from God our Father, and from the Lord Jesus Christ"*. Yet again I want to drive home the consequences of this statement, that being, Jesus is not linked to the term God, but rather is distinct from it. This once more shows the recurrent expression as to who Paul recognized God to be and who the messiah is.

Bringing the focus specifically to this text, in this greeting the use of the term God is seen six times, with two unequivocally saying the Father is God, the first two being mentioned above. Another one of the six times Paul writes *"I thank my God...for the grace of God which is given you in Christ Jesus"*. The term God refers back to *"God our Father"*, seeing it can in no way indicate anyone else according to the context. So contextually it should be understood he is saying *"I thank God (my) Father...* The motivation he has for giving thanks is *"the grace...given you in Christ Jesus"*[58], asserting that Jesus is the means through which we receive grace from Him (God). Paul makes it clear that the grace spoken of is given by his God <u>in</u>[59] Christ.

---

[58] thus, continuing with the absence of God being applied to Jesus
[59] This is another example showing the numerous ways **διά** is

Paul's final words from this passage read *"God is faithful, by whom you were called to the fellowship of His Son Jesus Christ our Lord"*.

I find it extremely difficult for Jesus to be God seeing that God called us into fellowship with him[60]. It stands then that God is the Father of Jesus just as He is to us. This leaves Jesus independent from the person of God. I must stress the fact that whether he uses *God*, *God the Father* or *God our Father*, it invariably speaks of the same person, that being Jesus' and our God and Father.

6. *Paul, an apostle of Jesus Christ by the will of God, and Timothy our brother, to the church of God which is at Corinth, with all the saints which are in all Achaia: Grace be to you and peace from God our Father, and from the Lord Jesus Christ. Blessed be the God and Father of our Lord Jesus Christ, the Father of mercies, and the God of all comfort; Who comforts us in all our tribulation, that we may be able to comfort them which are in any trouble, by the comfort with which we ourselves are comforted of God.—2Corinthians 1:1-4*

As has been mentioned earlier, Paul was chosen by the will of God to be an apostle. What intrigues when he mentions this is that he was to be an apostle of Jesus. This would be quite an odd statement had he

---

translated. I would suggest that *through* would be a more appropriate word to use seeing it would give a better understanding of what is taking place

[60] Jesus

understood Jesus to have been God, seeing God chose him to be his apostle. This clearly shows, it was not Jesus's will, but Gods. This could only imply someone other than Jesus is God.

The opening of Paul's greeting reads *"peace from God our Father and..."* I believe punctuation is necessary here to clarify something very important. So, it would read *"from God, our Father, and (from) Jesus Christ, our lord"*. Scripture is quite clear, God is our Father, as even Jesus consistently says, as seen here, *"true worshipers will worship the Father in spirit and truth, for the Father is seeking such people to worship Him. God is spirit, and those who worship Him must worship in spirit and truth"*.[61] The words directly following verse three of first Corinthians affirm this stating *"Blessed be the God and Father of our Lord Jesus Christ"*. Additionally, Paul writes these very same words later in this epistle, *"the God and Father of the Lord Jesus, He who is blessed forever, knows that I am not lying."*[62] This validates what is being presented.

Moreover, within these verses of scripture the apostle joins together with *the God and Father of Jesus* that He is also the *"the Father of mercies, God of all comfort"* along with *"He who is blessed forever"*.

Considering his mentioning of the *Father of mercies* I would presume he is referring to the

---

[61] John 4:24-25
[62] 2Corinthians 11:31

Almighty's description of Himself in Exodus chapter thirty-three verse nineteen, *"I will make all my goodness pass before you and will proclaim before you my name 'YHWH.' And I will be gracious to whom I will be gracious, and will show mercy on whom I will show mercy"*, while his use of *"God of all comfort"* reminds me of the Psalms, such as *"let, I pray you, your merciful kindness be for my comfort, according to your word to your servant"*[63]. It is also important to note that when Jesus is referred to it says of him that he is *"the lord"* who has a God, that being the/his Father.

With all of this laid out, we have here overwhelming evidence that decisively shows no one but the Father of our lord Jesus Christ can be the God of scripture. Unless we can conclude Jesus is our Father as well, there is no connection whatsoever with his person to the title God. God is only used in association with the Father, there is no exception whatsoever.

7. *Paul, an apostle, (not of men, neither by man, but by Jesus Christ, and God the Father, who raised him from the dead ;) And all the brothers which are with me, to the churches of Galatia: Grace be to you and peace from God our Father, and from our Lord Jesus Christ, Who gave himself for our sins, that he might deliver us from this present evil world, according to the will of our God and Father: To*

---

[63] Psalm 119:76

whom be glory for ever and ever. Amen.—Galatians 1:1-5

In just this short passage the apostle speaks of God being our Father, as he so often does. But what makes this passage even more clear concerning the personhood of God is his statement *our God and Father*. In this brief statement the one whom determined that Jesus give his life to deliver us, is both said to be our God and our Father. With this in mind, it would seem obvious, I hope, that Jesus cannot be our God and Father. For him giving himself was according to the will of this other distinct being. Speaking of this, Jesus gives us this same testimony saying *"no man takes it from me, but I lay it down of myself. I have power to lay it down, and I have power to take it again. This commandment have I received of my Father"*[64]. It is because of this great grace given to us that Paul declares it is to our God and Father there *be glory forever and ever.*

I also think it to be important to note the three references to God in this passage, those being, *God the Father, God our Father, and our God and Father*. I believe one can conclude from the context of this passage that these all refer to the same person, the Father. That would make it clear then that when one reads *God the Father*, it can be alternated with *God our Father* and *our God and Father*. This fact

---

[64] John 10:13

insists that if one is not our Father, they cannot be our God.

If the reader will take the plain evidence I have presented, scripture without question declares that our Father and the Father of Jesus, is the God who unaidedly determined the plan for delivering us from this evil world.

8. *Paul, an apostle of Jesus Christ by the will of God, to the saints which are at Ephesus, and to the faithful in Christ Jesus: Grace be to you, and peace, from God our Father, and from the Lord Jesus Christ. Blessed be the God and Father of our Lord Jesus Christ, who has blessed us with all spiritual blessings in heavenly places in Christ: According as he has chosen us in him before the foundation of the world, that we should be holy and without blame before him in love: Having predestinated us to the adoption of children by Jesus Christ to himself, according to the good pleasure of his will, To the praise of the glory of his grace, wherein he has made us accepted in the beloved.—Ephesians 1:1-6*

It is remarkable how Paul, time after time, declares in the opening of his epistles who God is. One would think this would be adequate to conclude who the apostle understood to be God. Yet, despite the explicit and obvious conclusion placed before us, the majority cannot or will not see it.

This can be found in this passage in the second half of the first sentence, *"Grace be to you, and peace, from God our Father, and from the Lord Jesus Christ"*. Though he has unequivocally described who God is, that being our Father, the evidence does not stop there. He gives us even more assurance of His identity by saying *"blessed be the God and Father of our Lord Jesus Christ"*. Him speaking of God being our Father and this same person being the God and Father of Jesus, is clearly seen in the masters' own words found in John's gospel, *"go to my brothers and say to them, 'I am ascending to my Father and your Father, to my God and your God."*[65]

He further continues by explaining what the God and Father of our lord Jesus Christ has done for us, that being that *"He has blessed us with all spiritual blessings…according as He has chosen us in him…that we should be…holy before Him…having predestined us… to Himself, according…to His will…His grace…has made us accepted"*.

Here Paul distinctly tells us it is the Fathers will[66], which is significant because it correlates with what Jesus teaches in Matthew chapter six verses nine through fifteen to pray that the Father's will be done *"on earth as it is in heaven"*. It is astonishing to find that none of these things are equated to be the will or purpose of any other person than the *"God and Father of our lord Jesus"*.

---

[65] John 20:17
[66] He, Him, Himself, and His are all in connection with the Father only

I am not quite sure how anyone can come away from this and still hold to the belief that another person, or persons, can be equally God with the Father in any way. For there is no place which suggests such a doctrine. If indeed it were so, there would no doubt be evidence that the determining of these things would not just be credited to the Father.

9. *For this cause I bow my knees to the Father of our Lord Jesus Christ, Of whom the whole family in heaven and earth is named, That he would grant you, according to the riches of his glory, to be strengthened with might by his Spirit in the inner man; That Christ may dwell in your hearts by faith; that you, being rooted and grounded in love, May be able to comprehend with all the saints what is the breadth, and length, and depth, and height; And to know the love of Christ, which passes knowledge, that you might be filled with all the fullness of God. Now to him that is able to do exceeding abundantly above all that we ask or think, according to the power that works in us, To him be glory in the church by Christ Jesus throughout all ages, world without end. Amen.—Ephesians 3:14-21*

This passage is a continuation from the epistle to the Ephesians and is found in later chapters after the verses that were looked at previously.

Just as chapter one, there is a great deal of evidence here to verify what I am presenting is the proper picture of who God is. Here, Paul gives to us a very revealing statement about this subject as he writes, *"the Father of our Lord Jesus Christ, of whom the whole family in heaven and earth is named"*. This statement the *Father of...Jesus* is definitely speaking of the same being described as *the God and Father of...Jesus* in chapter one, who will repeatedly be seen as our God and Father throughout the New Testament as well. The statement connected with this informs us that the God spoken of, is the one *"of whom the whole family in heaven and earth is named"*. The previously discussed passage explains for us that *"the God and Father of our lord Jesus ...predestined us to the adoption of children"*, thus including us in *"the whole family in heaven and earth"* (though we are so as well by being created in His image). This is the one who Paul bows his knee to *"that He would grant you, according to the riches of His glory, to be strengthened with might by His Spirit in the inner man"*[67]. This apostle expresses this very same being to be the one that *"is able to do exceeding abundantly above all that we ask or think, according to the power that works in us, to Him be glory in the church by Christ Jesus throughout all ages, world without end. Amen"*, and later in this epistle he urges us to give *"thanks always and for everything to God the Father in the name of our Lord Jesus Christ"*[68]. In his finishing words within this letter, Paul tells the

---

[67] This is an example of the Spirit not being understood to be a person, but rather the power of God, for it says "that He would grant you to be...strengthened with might by His Spirit"

[68] Ephesians 5:20—Young's Literal Translation

church that he desires what he greeted them with, that there be *"Peace unto the brethren, and love with faith, from God our Father, and Lord Jesus Christ"*[69].

To sum this up, I want to remind the reader of what is a common catch phrase among believers in the messiah, "let scripture interpret itself". I encourage that this suggestion be heeded, otherwise we attempt to build a puzzle with the wrong pieces.

10. *Paul and Timothy, servants of Christ Jesus, to all the saints in Christ Jesus who are at Philippi, with the overseers and deacons: Grace to you and peace from God our Father and the Lord Jesus Christ. I thank my God in all my remembrance of you, always in every prayer of mine for you all making my prayer with joy, because of your partnership in the gospel from the first day until now. And I am sure of this, that he who began a good work in you will bring it to completion at the day of Jesus Christ. It is right for me to feel this way about you all, because I hold you in my heart, for you are all partakers with me of grace, both in my imprisonment and in the defense and confirmation of the gospel. For God is my witness, how I yearn for you all with the affection of Christ Jesus. And it is my prayer that your love may abound more and more, with knowledge and all discernment, so that you may approve what is excellent, and so be pure and blameless for the day of Christ, filled with the fruit of righteousness that*

---

[69] Ephesians 6:23—Rotherhams's Emphasized Bible

comes through Jesus Christ, to the glory and praise of God.—Philippians 1:1-11

I want to bring up something here I have not addressed to this point. Quite often when Paul opens his epistles, of which most contain the phrase *"God our Father"* (which is in contrast to *the Lord Jesus Christ*) in relation to grace and peace, he also gives thanks, as he does here, to his God. Considering he just said God is our Father, as opposed to Jesus being our lord, it would seem quite odd, without clearly stating it, to suppose him to equate the personhood of God in the following chapters to someone other than *our Father*.

The next thought I want to share leads us to a very well know verse found in this passage, *"He who began a good work in you will bring it to completion"*. In this verse many assume that *He* refers to Jesus. But this cannot be the case. The reason being the apostle finishes this thought by saying that it will take place *"at the day of Jesus Christ"*[70]. This causes an obvious problem if indeed the *He* refers to Jesus. That is because the *He* that began the work will do so until it is complete at Jesus's return. In him wording it this way the apostle shows that *He* must be directing us back to the person from the statement *I thank my God*, which must be the one *who began a good work* and *will bring it to completion*.

---

[70] This statement is made twice in this passage and later in 2:16

Furthermore, as Paul finishes this passage there is more evidence found supporting this as he writes *"the fruit of righteousness that comes through Jesus Christ, to the glory and praise of God"*. Certainly, one could not believe the words God and Jesus are being applied to the same person? This clearly speaks of two different persons, that being God and Jesus. Seeing then there are two persons referred to, the question must be, is God doing the work, or is Jesus doing it, for his use of *He* does not allow for both. Logically, from the evidence the resolution as to who is doing and will finish the work can be none other than the one he clearly identifies as *God our Father.*

Looking at the statement *"to the glory and praise of God"*, we can find this notion of glory being given to God because of, or through Jesus several times in the New Testament. Some examples are; *"to the only wise God be glory forevermore through Jesus Christ! Amen"*,[71] *"every tongue confess that Jesus Christ is Lord, to the glory of God the Father"*[72], and *"that God in all things may be glorified through Jesus Christ, to whom be praise and dominion for ever and ever. Amen"*[73]. These verses unquestionably reveal that God as a singular person cannot be Jesus, because it is God the Father that will receive the glory. This is significant because Jesus speaks often of the Father giving him or others glory or receiving

---

[71] Romans 16:27
[72] Philippians 2:11
[73] 1 Peter 4:11

glory from the works of others.[74] This being said, God in this statement can refer only to the Father.

11. *Therefore God has highly exalted him and bestowed on him the name that is above every name, so that at the name of Jesus every knee should bow, in heaven and on earth and under the earth, and every tongue confess that Jesus Christ is Lord, to the glory of God the Father.*

—Philippians 2:9-11

This passage is located in the above-mentioned letter, so understandably the term God would also be applied to the same person here. The opening words of this passage support even further this fact as the apostle says, *"God has highly exalted him and bestowed on him the name that is above every name"*. Seeing that Jesus is the one exalted by God, it would be illogical to determine he or any other being can be the one who is responsible for exalting him.

Moreover, the apostle clearly shows that his name was given by someone greater than himself[75], which is the same being who exalted him. Another important factor that is noteworthy is that the God who exalted him and gave Jesus this name is also responsible for every knee bowing to him and confessing he is lord[76], which seems strange if indeed he is God himself.

---

[74] Matthew 5:16, 16:27, Mark 8:38, Luke 9:26, John 5:44, 7:18, 8:54, 12:43, 17:22, 24

[75] Matthew 1:21

In the ending words of the passage, we find that this is all done *"to the glory of God the Father"*. In these words, the apostle is referring back to the God who did all of the things mentioned in this text and that He did it to His own glory, and not another. A very similar statement is found in first Corinthians chapter fifteen *"Then comes the end, when he delivers the kingdom to God the Father after destroying every rule and every authority and power, for he must reign until he has put all his enemies under his feet... When all things are subjected to him, then the Son himself will also be subjected to him who put all things in subjection under him, that God may be all in all"*.[77]

So then, the ultimate end of what the messiah has accomplished is the Father being all in all.

In conclusion, the outcome of examining this passage is in full agreement with those displayed in all of the previously offered examples, there is no other God than ours and our messiahs Father.

12. *And my God will supply every need of yours according to His riches in glory in Christ Jesus. To our God and Father be glory forever and ever. Amen.—Philippians 4:19-20*

---

[76] Lord in relation to Jesus should be understood to mean he is the messiah and the one who was prophesied to reign on the throne of David

[77] 1 Corinthians 15:24-25, 28

More convincing evidence is seen in these verses which again describe who our God is. What makes this even more significant is that these verses occur within the same epistle as the two aforementioned portions. That being said, the foundation for the exposition of this text has already been laid, that being *God* is refer-ring to the Father.

At the outset of what is before us, there is the common principal of God doing something through Jesus. This is explained by the opening verse which says, *"my God will supply every need of yours according to His riches in glory in Christ Jesus."* The first piece of information that is essential to further explain this is Paul writing *"my God"* and *"His riches."* It is obvious that *God* and *His* are speaking of the same person, making this to be understood as *"God's riches."*

Following this he writes *in Christ Jesus*, which shows the means by which God supplies our needs. Thus, it is God's riches and not Jesus'.

Then in the very next verse Paul gives what should be an obvious explanation of who he identifies as *my God*. This can be seen in the succeeding words of the verse, *"to our God and Father"*. Seeing that Paul says *our God* in this verse, logically it can be concluded that when he says *my God* in verse nineteen, the same per-son is being referred to, which would be the Father. What is more, we can see in the words of Jesus himself this exact same idea as he says, *"do not cling to me, for I have not yet ascended to the Father; but go to my brothers and say to them, 'I am ascending to my Father and your Father, to my God and your God"*[78]. Here, as well as with what Paul writes, Jesus states *"my God and your God"*. Naturally, this can only be understood to mean *Father and God* is Jesus's *Father and God*.

In ending these verses, the apostle declares *"be all glory forever and ever, Amen"*. These words can be found in several of the other epistles of Paul, such as Galatians chapter one verses four through five," according *to the will of our God and Father, to whom be the glory forever and ever. Amen"*[79].

This should leave no doubt whatsoever that our God and Father alone is the one who supplies our every need and also is the architect of the plan to save whosoever will believe.

13. *Paul, an apostle of Christ Jesus by the will of God, and Timothy our brother, To the saints and faithful brothers in Christ at Colossae: Grace to you and peace from God our Father. We always thank God, the Father of our Lord Jesus Christ, when we pray for you—Colossians 1:1-3*

Paul, as he does many times, assures us it is by the will of God that he is an apostle. So, who is the person who willed Paul to be an apostle? I'll start with the words of Jesus in determining this, *"not*

---

[78] John 20:17
[79] Galatians 1:4-5

everyone that saith unto me, Lord, Lord, shall enter into the kingdom of heaven; but he that doeth the will of my Father who is in heaven"[80]. With this statement Jesus makes it clear that his Father is the one who's will is to be obeyed. Thus, it is the Father who is the God who willed that Paul be an apostle.

Taking this information into account, the following words give the reader a reliable portrayal of who the God that anointed Paul is, *"we always thank God, the Father of our Lord Jesus Christ"*. Touching on Paul giving thanks to God, our lords Father, scripture also gives mention of Jesus proclaiming *"I thank you, O Father, Lord of heaven and earth, because you have hid these things from the wise and prudent, and have revealed them to babes. Even so, Father: for so it seemed good in your sight"*[81].

There can be no dispute that the God who chose Paul to be an Apostle is the Father and God of Jesus as he himself and Paul confirm.

It should also be noticed, as has been said numerous times already, the apostle expresses that God is our Father. What's more, I want to point to what the Messiah tells Mary, *"touch me not; for I am not yet ascended unto the Father: but go unto my brethren, and say to them, I ascend unto my Father and your Father, and my God and your God"*[82]. Therefore, there can be no other person than the

---

[80] Matthew 7:21—King James Version
[81] Matthew 11:25-26
[82] John 20:17—*King James Version*

Father of our Messiah who is YHWH, the God of scripture.

14. *Paul, Silvanus, and Timothy, To the church of the Thessalonians in God the Father and the Lord Jesus Christ: Grace to you and peace. We give thanks to God always for all of you, constantly mentioning you in our prayers, remembering before our God and Father your work of faith and labor of love and steadfastness of hope in our Lord Jesus Christ. For we know, brothers loved by God, that he has chosen you, because our gospel came to you not only in word, but also in power and in the Holy Spirit and with full conviction. You know what kind of men we proved to be among you for your sake. And you became imitators of us and of the Lord, for you received the word in much affliction, with the joy of the Holy Spirit, so that you became an example to all the believers in Macedonia and in Achaia. For not only has the word of the Lord sounded forth from you in Macedonia and Achaia, but your faith in God has gone forth everywhere, so that we need not say anything. For they themselves report concerning us the kind of reception we had among you, and how you turned to God from idols to serve the living and true God, and to wait for his Son from heaven, whom he raised from the dead, Jesus, who delivers us from the wrath to come.* 1Thessalonians 1:1-10

This is one of only two or three of Paul's epistles that do not say *"grace and Peace from God our Father and Jesus Christ our Lord"*. Even though this is the case, it does not change the idea within what the apostle says here, that is, God is our Father.

In the opening of this letter two separate people are mentioned that grace and peace are received in[83], who are God the Father and the Lord Jesus Christ. This is consistent with the rest of scripture and shows with no obscurity that Jesus is our lord and Messiah, not our God.

In the next mention of God, the apostle speaks of giving thanks and prayer to this being. So, to whom is he giving thanks and praying to? We find the answer to this from reading his words that he was *"remembering before our God and Father your work of faith"*. The idea of praying to the Father, who Paul tells us is our God, is taught to us by Jesus himself who said *"pray then like this: "Our Father in heaven, hallowed be your name"*[84].

As the passage continues these disciples in Colossae are reminded of the beautiful testimony that they *"turned to God from idols to serve the living and true God"*. Once more we see the words *"true God"*, which point us back to John chapter seventeen verse three and Jude verse twenty-five.

As we continue reading in Colossians *the living and true God* can be identified by Paul saying *"and to wait for His Son from heaven, whom He raised*

---

[83] This is referring to grace and peace being receive through God the Father and Jesus Christ
[84] Matthew 6:9

from the dead. The fact that Jesus is God's son goes without question, but that in itself should be enough proof that His Father is God alone. But the important thing to recognize here is that Jesus is said not only to be His son but was raised by Him. So that can mean nothing other than *the living and true God* is Jesus' Father and He raised him from the dead. So, unquestionably this can refer to only one person, the Father.

Thus, from this passage it is seen once again that the true God is the Father of Jesus and is our God and Father as well.

15. *For what thanksgiving can we return to God for you, for all the joy that we feel for your sake before our God...Now may our God and Father himself, and our Lord Jesus, direct our way to you, and may the Lord make you increase and abound in love for one another and for all, as we do for you, so that he may establish your hearts blameless in holiness before our God and Father, at the coming of our Lord Jesus with all his saints.—1 Thessalonians 3:11-13*

Paul here pens down twice, *"our God and Father"*, and twice *"our lord Jesus"*.

In the opening words he does not only write *"our God and Father"*, but *"may our God...Himself"*, which is followed by *"and our lord"*. It must logically be gathered then that our God Himself can be none other than *our Father*. This fact is strengthened when *"and our lord"* follows, meaning they are two different persons, *our God*, and *our lord*. This gives a clear definition as to whom we are to understand God to be in his statement *"for what thanksgiving can we return to God for you, for all the joy that we feel for your sake before our God"*.

The desire Paul has for the readers of this letter is that they increase in love toward all, *"that he[85] may establish your hearts blameless...before our God and Father"*. The son is said here to be establishing us before our God. So, I find it quite impossible that if he is doing this before our God, that he himself is God. Therefore, it is evident that our Father is our God apart from any other person or being.

16. *Paul, Silvanus, and Timothy, To the church of the Thessalonians in God our Father and the Lord Jesus Christ: Grace to you and peace from God our Father and the Lord Jesus Christ. We ought always to give thanks to God for you, brothers, as is right, be-cause your faith is growing abundantly, and the love of every one of you for one another is increasing. Therefore we ourselves boast about you in the churches of God for your steadfastness and faith in all your persecutions and in the afflictions that you are enduring. This is evidence of the righteous judgment of God, that you may be considered worthy of the kingdom of God, for which you are also suffering since indeed God considers it*

---

[85] Jesus

just to repay with affliction those who afflict you, and to grant relief to you who are afflicted as well as to us, when the Lord Jesus is revealed from heaven with his mighty angels in flaming fire, inflicting vengeance on those who do not know God and on those who do not obey the gospel of our Lord Jesus. They will suffer the punishment of eternal destruction, away from the presence of the Lord and from the glory of his might, when he comes on that day to be glorified in his saints, and to be marveled at among all who have believed, because our testimony to you was believed.

To this end we always pray for you, that our God may make you worthy of his calling and may fulfill every resolve for good and every work of faith by his power, so that the name of our Lord Jesus may be glorified in you, and you in him, according to the grace of our God and the Lord Jesus Christ.—2 Thessalonians 1:1-12

We find in this passage the phrases *God our Father* and *our God* each stated twice, with all four separated from Jesus by the conjunction *and*. The two times the apostle writes *God our Father* are within the first sentence, the first instance, *"to the church…in God our Father"*, the second *"grace and peace from God our Father"*. The first occurrence helps to clarify something Jesus says in John's gospel, *"I do not ask for these only, but also for those who will believe in me through their word, that they may all be one, just as you, Father, are in me, and I in you, that they also may be in us, so that the world may believe that you have sent me"*[86]. This verse in Thessalonians shows us this in action, showing that the Father mentioned by Jesus is our God, thus we abide in our God and our Lord Jesus Christ, negating the possibility of the Father sharing His deity with anyone else. Just a few words later he pens the exact same words that bring about the same conclusion as above.

Looking further into the passage, there is a reference to grace that also helps to clear away the possible confusion, *"the grace of our God"*. When Jesus is joined to these statements his title, *"the Lord Jesus Christ"*, does not change. Hence, we can see Paul does not just say *"God our Father and"*, but here *"our God and"* gives us grace. Seeing that God is our Father, it can only logically be concluded that He alone is our God. This can also be bolstered through the apostle's words from Ephesians chapter three, *"For this reason I bow my knees before the Father, from whom every family in heaven and on earth is named"*[87]. Therefore, though we do receive grace from Jesus, The Father is singularly associated with the term God.

Another important point to make is whom is being extoled as the one being glorified for this work. In relation to this we find the apostle say: *"the righteous judgment of God"*, *"the kingdom of God"*,

---
[86] John 17:20-21
[87] Ephesians 3:14-15

"God considers it just to repay", and *"our God may make you worthy... by his power"*. Thus, it is God, and not Jesus, who is referred in these proclamations.

Now, touching on the judgment of God and His justice to repay, we find this will be accomplished *"when the Lord Jesus is revealed from heaven"*. Thus, we find that Jesus will be the medium through which God will judge[88], which the apostles said of him in Acts chapter ten verse forty-two, *"he commanded us to preach to the people and to testify that he is the one appointed by God to be judge of the living and the dead"*. I find it extremely unintelligible to suppose the one appointed by God, to himself be God.

With all of this considered, other than the Father, there is no connection with any other person when using the term God in this passage.

17. *But we ought always to give thanks to God for you, brothers beloved by the Lord, because God chose you as the first fruits to be saved, through sanctification by the Spirit and belief in the truth. To this he called you through our gospel, so that you may obtain the glory of our Lord Jesus Christ. So then, brothers, stand firm and hold to the traditions that you were taught by us, either by our spoken word or by our letter. Now may our Lord Jesus Christ himself, and God our Father, who loved us and gave us eternal comfort and good hope through grace,*

---

[88] Also see 2Timothy 4:1

comfort your hearts and establish them in every good work and word. —2 Thessalonians 2:13-17

It has already been established that when the singular term *God* is used, it is speaking of the Father, which was shown previously in the first chapter of this letter. That being demonstrated, we can apply that to its use here as well.

The opening statement given by Paul, *"we ought always to give thanks to God"*, are the exact words used in verse three of chapter one. Seeing then that the term *God* is referenced to *our Father,* this would allow these words to be used interchangeably. So, this could just as easily say *"but we ought always to give thanks to God our Father*, which can also be applied to the statement that follows, *"God chose you as the first fruits to be saved"*. Because of this when Paul writes *"He called you"*, it should be understood that *He* is speaking of the God who called us, which has been shown to be our Father.

We are then told what we are called to, that being to *"obtain the glory of our Lord Jesus Christ"*. There-fore, the use of *He called* makes it clear that *our lord* is not the God who called us, nor is he the God Paul gives thanks to.

Speaking of *the glory of our lord* we are called to obtain; the Messiah alludes to this saying, *"the glory that you have given me I have given to them that they may be one even as we are one"*[89].

---

[89] Matthew 6:9

We find today that most of those who deny the concept of a true Monotheistic theology[90], have conceived the notion that when the word *glory* is associated with Jesus, that it refers to the glory of the Al-mighty. The "proof text" used to justify this ridiculous invention says *"...My glory I will not give to another"*[91]. If someone looks at this critically, they will see the context this is spoken in, *"for My name's sake I will put off My anger; and for My praise I will hold back for you, so as not to cut you off. Behold, I have refined you, but not with silver; I have chosen you in the furnace of affliction. For My sake, for My sake, I will act; for how is it defiled"*[92]. It should be understood then that this is associated with something He (God) does, and He will not allow anyone but Himself to be glorified in the doing of it. Thus, they ignore how the word is used in a passage, in addition to disregarding the different applications of glory in our English Bibles. To limit a word in such a way causes a great deal of confusion.

A demonstration of the difficulty caused by this theory is found in John's gospel which says *"this he said about the Spirit, whom those who believed in him were to receive, for as yet the Spirit had not been*

---

[90] The only Monotheistic religion in the world that supports a multiple person God is Christianity. But that concept rejects the definition of Monotheism itself. The attempt to support this is to argue that though He is three persons He is still one God, which actually is one essence, which is how they define God as a whole. *Three persons one essence* or as some say *three persons one being*

[91] Isaiah 48:11

[92] Isaiah 48: 9-11

given, because Jesus was not yet glorified"[93]. In this we can see until the resurrection he had not been glorified yet.

Another Evidence of this is seen in Jesus's own words *"Father, the hour has come; glorify your Son that the Son may glorify you"*[94]. In this instance the Messiah has requested to receive this glory, which John seven tells us does not happen until his resurrection. The fulfilment of him receiving this glory can be seen in Acts chapter three verse thirteen which reads *"the God of Abraham, the God of Isaac, and the God of Jacob, the God of our fathers, glorified his servant Jesus, whom you delivered over and denied in the presence of Pilate, when he had decided to release him"*. Through this we can see glory was given to him when he was raised from the dead because he did *"always do the things that are pleasing to Him"*, thus it was not inherently his[95].

Furthermore, in Jesus's words *"they loved the glory that comes from man more than the glory that comes from God"*[96] we are shown that men can receive glory from God, as well as from men. How then is this word defined and how are we to know how it is used?

The way the word is used in the New Testament, Thayer's Lexicon defines it as: *opinion, estimate,*

---

[93] John 7:39
[94] John 17:1
[95] John 8:29
[96] John 12:43

whether good or bad concerning someone; in the NT always a good opinion concerning one, resulting in praise, honor and glory[97]. Basically, it means that one who performs in an acceptable and pleasing manner in his actions will be honored and praised. I am sure some people may say "praised! God praise and honor us, blaspheme!" It is however taught to us in scripture.

In Romans chapter two and verse seven the apostle Paul tells us that *"those who by patience in well-doing seek for glory and honor and immortality, he will give eternal life"*. So, are we to seek what we cannot truly obtain? Clearly Paul tells us we can receive glory from God through the Messiah if we *"continue in the faith, stable and steadfast, not shifting from the hope of the gospel that you heard, which has been proclaimed in all creation under heaven"*. But on the other hand, we are told by Jesus that we will not receive this glory if we seek the praises of men. So, the glory Jesus possesses is not the glory that YHWH Himself possesses, just as the glory the faithful will receive is not.

As we have moved through this passage the differentiation between these persons has become progressively more noticeable.

In Paul's ending words, the picture is completed as we find the last mention of these individuals when

---

[97] *Thayer's Greek-English Lexicon of the New Testament; Joseph Thayer*

he writes *"now may our Lord Jesus Christ himself, and God our Father, who loved us and gave us eternal comfort and good hope through grace"*. Once more, the separation that is repeatedly caused by the addition of the conjunction *and* between *Jesus Christ* and *God our Father* surfaces again. In this case though, the wording is much more precise than many of the other texts. In this instance he writes *our Lord Jesus Christ himself,* with the use of *himself* clearly making him a singular self. Furthermore, when he says *God our Father,* we now undoubtedly have two different singular self's, one being our lord Jesus and the other being our Father who is God. He then follows this by saying *"who loved us and gave us eternal comfort and good hope through grace"*. This statement cannot even be implied to be something that Jesus did, but rather from God our Father. Therefore, the God to whom he gives thanks and the God who called us is our Father *"who loved us and gave us eternal comfort and good hope through grace"*.

There can be no interpretation except that the title God is always referring to our Father in this passage, thus, once again showing He alone is God.

18. *Paul, an apostle of Christ Jesus by command of God our Savior and of Christ Jesus our hope, To Timothy, my true child in the faith: : Grace, mercy, peace, from God our Father and Christ Jesus our Lord.—1Timothy 1:1-2*

As Paul does in the majority of his letters, he tells us he is chosen to be an apostle by God, saying, *"the command of God our Savior"*.

It is an undisputable fact that God (YHWH) is our savior. But the New Testament also proclaims that Jesus is our savior, which many use as a proof of a multi-person God. But this is not the case. The Old Testament speaks of many saviors, usually referring to the book of Judges. Nehemiah testifies to this saying *"Therefore you gave them into the hand of their enemies, who made them suffer. And in the time of their suffering they cried out to you and you heard them from heaven, and according to your great mercies you gave them saviors who saved them from the hand of their enemies"*.[98] It is in this way that Jesus is our savior, just as John writes in his first epistle *"And we have seen and testify that the Father has sent his Son to be the Savior of the world"*.[99]

We can also find this illustrated in Acts chapter five verse thirty-one which says, *"Of this man's offspring God has brought to Israel a Savior, Jesus, as he promised"*. Thus, it is not necessary for Jesus to be God in order to be our savior.

The apostle also sheds more light on Jesus being described as savior by calling him *our hope*. This is in contrast to *God our Savior*, showing once more that the title God is not connected to Jesus. From this

---

[98] Nehemiah 9:27
[99] 1 John 4:14

we can deduce that our hope is in Jesus, whom God sent to save us, allowing for not only God to be our savior, but Jesus as well. This reveals that they both play different parts in the fulfillment of this, God is our savior, of whom John said, *"God so loved the world he gave"*, and Jesus is our savior by being the means in which God accomplishes His plan of salvation.

Paul then says in first Timothy *"grace, mercy, peace, from God our Father and Christ Jesus our Lord"*. In this statement it is confirmed that God is the Father by using the wording *God our* as he so often does. This conclusion is further reached through his beginning statement *God our Savior*.

He then writes in his final words of this passage *Christ Jesus our Lord* which he once more differentiates from *God our Father* by the conjunction *and* yet again. Additionally, the relationship that the word *our* has with these statements is also seen in those listed previously, *God our Savior* and *Jesus our hope*. Each of these shows who God is and who/what Jesus is. Through these facts we can conclusively assess that God is our Savior and our Father whereas Jesus is our hope and our lord. The end result can be nothing other than the Father is God alone.

19. *Paul, an apostle of Christ Jesus by the will of God according to the promise of the life that is in Christ Jesus, To Timothy, my beloved child: Grace, mercy, and peace from God our Father and Christ*

Jesus our Lord. I thank God whom I serve, as did my ancestors, with a clear conscience, as I remember you constantly in my prayers night and day.— 2Timothy 1:1-2

Yet again Paul contrasts the actions and results associated with God and Jesus. This is seen when he says he is *"an apostle of Christ Jesus by the will of God"*, as well as the statement *"the promise of life that is in Christ Jesus"*[100].

In the first he declares he is an apostle because God called him to this position, while in the second the promise of life is given because of Jesus. These statements explain who chose Paul to be an apostle and why, which are the action and results I was referring to. Here again is the conjunction, and that has repeatedly been spoken of differentiating the two persons.

In this passage is a very similar situation that is contained in a majority of Paul's epistles. He greets us with *grace, mercy and peace from God our Father* which is also given through *Christ Jesus our lord*, which obviously shows once more that God is our Father, whereas Jesus is our lord.

The thing I want to emphasize is his use of *God* in this passage. Those being *the will of God, God our*

---

[100] On an aside, when looking at the statement *the promise of life that is in Christ Jesus,* the apostle reveals why Jesus is our hope as he said in first Timothy, that being through him we are promised eternal life.

Father, and *I thank God.* Considering he has already said in his greeting that Jesus is our lord, it seems reasonable to conclude that his use of the term *God* can only refer to the person he clearly says is God, who would be our Father. This can further be proven by studying the idea of the *will of God*. The most convincing proof that this is correct comes from Jesus's own words as he teaches us to pray, *"... May your will be done, on earth as it is in heaven"*[101]. Concerning this it is written of the Messiah *"Then I said, 'Behold, I have come to do your will, O God, as it is written of me in the scroll of the book"*[102] of which he agrees saying *"...I always do the things that are pleasing to Him"*[103] and again *"I do as the Father has commanded me..."*[104]. In addition to this, I find these words of Paul very helpful as well *"I thank God whom I serve, as did my ancestors"*. This reason being, numerous verses referring to the God of his ancestors as the source of things done for Jesus. Two of these can be seen in the book of Acts, *"The God of Abraham, the God of Isaac, and the God of Jacob, the God of our fathers, glorified his servant Jesus..."*[105] and another *"The God of our fathers raised Jesus, whom you killed by hanging him on a tree"*[106]. Thus,

---

[101] Matthew 6:10
[102] Psalms 40:7, Hebrews 10:7
[103] John 8:29
[104] John 14:21
[105] Acts 3:13
[106] Acts 5:30

the very God Paul calls our Father, is his God, and is the God of his ancestors.

When evidence is collected and tested, I find there can be no other position held than, the Father alone is our God.

20. *Paul, a servant of God and an apostle of Jesus Christ, for the sake of the faith of God's elect and their knowledge of the truth, which accords with godliness, in hope of eternal life, which God, who never lies, promised before the ages began and at the proper time manifested in His word through the preaching with which I have been entrusted by the command of God our Savior; To Titus, my true child in a common faith: Grace and peace from God the Father and Christ Jesus our Savior.—Titus 1:1-4*

As it has consistently been the case, Paul distinguishes between God, of whom he says he is a servant, and Jesus Christ, of whom he is an apostle, which once again is caused by the conjunction *and*. Therefore, the one he is a servant of and the one he is an apostle of are two separate persons. Along with this the apostle also gives another important fact saying, *"God who never lies"*. It is quite powerful that this would be seen in the midst of this greeting. The reason being, that if one wishes to make the accusation that someone along with the Father is God, they are calling Him a liar if He, God the Father, were to say the opposite. There is no legitimate argument that God can refer to someone other than the Father in this text. This is verified by the final words of this passage, *"grace and peace from God the Father…"*

Something noteworthy pertaining to this is seen in the Greek text which reads εἰρήνη ἀπὸ θεοῦ πατρὸς. I want the reader to be aware there is no definite article[107] linked to either word, so it would accurately read *"peace from God Father"*. *The* is added into the translation to make sense of it in English. But it can also be understood to say *"our Father"* instead of *"the Father"* because of this.

In order to determine how this should be translated what surrounds it has to be considered. The apostles use of *our* to explain whom Jesus is savior of, I believe, gives us the answer. Considering *our* is used when speaking of Jesus, I find it odd that *the* would be preferred over *our* seeing He is described in most of Paul's greetings as *"our Father"*. Rotherham's Emphasized Bible agrees with what I have said, though he rightly puts *our* in parenthesis.

An additional element that would help in making a clearer picture is to give a clearer translation of what is being said and add punctuation, such as *"from God, who is our Father, and Jesus Christ, who is our savior"*. In doing so we can clearly gather that God is our Father and Jesus Christ is our savior, two distinct positions and two individual persons.

Something that has been used in an attempt to refute what I have said comes from these words,

---

[107] The definite article is equivalent to our English word "the"

"Christ Jesus our savior". So, the question is, who is our savior, the Father or Jesus? The answer to that is both, but not because Jesus is God. On the contrary, because God[108] saves us through Jesus, as is seen in Romans chapter five verse ten, *"for if while we were enemies we were reconciled to God by the death of his Son, much more, now that we are reconciled, shall we be saved by his life"*.

This idea of men being saviors is not a new concept that only pertains to the Messiah. This reality can be seen many times in scripture such as Nehemiah, as I mentioned previously, which says *"therefore you gave them into the hand of their enemies, who made them suffer. And in the time of their suffering they cried out to you and you heard them from heaven, and according to your great mercies you gave them saviors who saved them from the hand of their enemies"*[109]. An example of this is seen in Judges chapter three verse nine, *"and the sons of Israel made outcry unto Yahweh, so Yahweh raised up a savior unto the sons of Israel, who saved them,—even Othniel son of Kenaz, Caleb's younger brother"*[110]. So, one does not have to be God to be a savior. They must only be willing to submit to YHWH's will.

The last point to be made is the use of the term God and those things associated with the being it

---

[108] The Father
[109] Nehemiah 9:27
[110] *Rotherham Emphasized Bible*

represents. They are as follows: *Servant of God, God's elect, God who never lies, His word, God our savior* and *God our Father.*

What I want to put the most emphasis on is the connection between *His word* and the *God who never lies*. From this we can ascertain that *the word* Paul is speaking of belongs to the *God who never lies*. Considering then that the only mention of a personal being that is called God refers to the Father, reason would tell us this is the *God who never lies*.

Certainly, some disagree with this, so I will give more evidence to substantiate my case. Jesus says this in John chapter seventeen verse seventeen, *"Sanctify them in the truth; your word is truth"*. Anyone who has read the gospel of John knows he is speaking to the Father when saying this. But what makes this so key to what I am presenting is what he says prior to this, that being *"...that they know you, the only true God..."*[111]

Thus, I find no other possible explanation according to scripture about who Paul is referring to than this; the Father is the only true God, who Paul serves preaching His word, who can never lie and is our savior. Any other interpretation would be unsubstantiated.

21. *Grace to you and peace from God our Father and the Lord Jesus Christ. I thank my God always when I remember you in my prayers, because I hear*

---
[111] John 17:3

of your love and of the faith that you have toward the Lord Jesus and for all the saints, and I pray that the sharing of your faith may become effective for the full knowledge of every good thing that is in us for the sake of Christ—Philemon 1:3-6

In these verses Paul refers to God in His relationship to the whole of the believers and to the individual. Of the whole he writes *"God our Father"*, whereas in connection with himself alone, he says *"my God"*.

When he speaks of giving thanks to God, it should already be understood that he is speaking of *God our Father*. He then gives his reason for giving thanks *"because of your love and of the faith that you have toward the Lord Jesus and for all the saints"*. Thus, he is giving thanks to his God[112] because of our love for Jesus. With that said, any other being is exempt from the God Paul is speaking of.

In Colossians this same idea is seen, *"we always thank God, the Father of our Lord Jesus Christ, when we pray for you, since we heard of your faith in Christ Jesus and of the love that you have for all the saints"*[113].

There are two differences in this text that strengthen what has been expounded on in Philemon to this point. The first point is the words *"we always thank God"*. Instead of him saying *"my God"*, as he

---

[112] Our Father
[113] Colossians 1:3-4

does in Philemon, he writes *"we...thank God"*, showing the God he gives thanks to in Philemon is the exact same God we see here in Colossians. But what Paul writes in Colossians next, *"the Father of our lord Jesus Christ"*, really closes the case. Not only does he give thanks to his and our God, we are also told that the same God that is our Father is the Father of Jesus as well.

Another small thing to point out is Paul's mention of prayer to God. We all know the Lord's Prayer very well, but it is whom Jesus says to pray to that is important, that being the Father. So that must mean that Paul, just as Jesus, is praying to the Father, of whom both say is their God.

Once more there can be no other conclusion, our Father is God just as Jesus's Father is God. The Father is God alone.

22. *Pure religion and undefiled before our God and Father is this, to visit the fatherless and widows in their affliction, and to keep oneself unspotted from the world.—James 1:27*

Here we are given more evidence showing that God is the Father alone as James writes *"our God **and** Father"*. That the conjunction *and* is used here is important. Not only do we read *God our Father* in the New Testament, but now we have *our God and Father*, just as Paul has stated several times as well. Unless we are to take this as "before our God, (the Father, the son and the holy spirit)", the only way this can be understood is that the very same person who is our God is also our Father, thus, our God is the Father.

An additional thing of importance is seen as James defines what pure and undefiled religion before our God and Father is, *"visit the fatherless and widows in their affliction"*. The reason this is important to this subject comes through the words of Jesus which takes this idea even further saying *"but love your enemies, and do good, and lend, expecting nothing in return, and your reward will be great, and you will be sons of the Most High, for he is kind to the ungrateful and the evil. Be merciful, even as your Father is merciful"*[114]. So, we are not to just visit the fatherless and widows as James says, but to be sons of the Most High, which, considering the use of sons, can only mean the Father is the Most High (unless Jesus has sons). This should be sufficient to show that the Most-High, our Father, is the *God and Father* of whom James is speaking of.

23. *According to the foreknowledge of God the Father, in the sanctification of the Spirit, for obedience to Jesus Christ and for sprinkling with his blood: May grace and peace be multiplied to you. Blessed be the God and Father of our Lord Jesus Christ! According to his great mercy, he has caused us to be born again to a living hope through the resurrection of Jesus Christ from the dead, to an*

---

[114] Luke 6:35-36

inheritance that is imperishable, undefiled, and unfading, kept in heaven for you, who by God's power are being guarded through faith for a salvation ready to be revealed in the last time— 1Peter 1:2-5

When scripture speaks of foreknowledge, it consistently is found that the only being which possess foreknowledge as a characteristic is the Father, just as the opening of this text reveals, *"the foreknowledge of God the Father"*.

Though many who support the deity of Jesus argue he had this foreknowledge as well, there is no such claim in scripture. But we most certainly find many times that he does and says what the Father tells him and knows beforehand that which the Father has make known to him for he was a prophet.

Continuing to the next verse Peter writes *"blessed be the God and Father of our Lord Jesus Christ"*. This statement can be found throughout the epistles, especially those of Paul, thus, strengthening the fact that the personhood of God is the Father alone. So, we find then, not only are we told the Father is the sole possessor of foreknowledge, but He is also given the designation of *"the God and Father of our lord Jesus"*.

Furthermore, Peter tells us why he blesses God the Father, that being because *"according to His great mercy, he has caused us to be born again to a living hope through the resurrection of Jesus Christ from the dead"*. The importance of this comes from him saying *"through the resurrection of Jesus"*, of which Peter later writes, *"...God...raised him from the dead and gave him glory, so that your faith and hope are in God"*[115]. This brings about a concrete assurance to my claim. For the Father isn't limited to the accolades and attributes stated above, but now is said to have raised Jesus from the dead, then gave him glory and all for the purpose of our hope resting in Him.

The reader should also notice Peters statements, *"His great mercy"*, *"He has caused us"*, and *"by Gods great power"*. Each of these refer back to when he says, *"the God and Father of our Lord Jesus Christ"*.

In addition to this, I would like to also mention something I have not discussed to this point, which is the fact that the Holy Spirit is never portrayed or even listed in any of the texts I have and will present implying it to be the "third person of the Trinity". This is the reason I have not and most likely will not spend time in addressing the claim of the personhood of the Spirit of God.

All of this said, we can realistically ascertain nothing other than the Father is God by Himself.

24. *For we did not follow cleverly devised myths when we made known to you the power and coming of our Lord Jesus Christ, but we were eyewitnesses of*

---

[115] 1Peter 1:21

his majesty. For when he received honor and glory from God the Father, and the voice was borne to him by the Majestic Glory, "This is my beloved Son, with whom I am well pleased," we ourselves heard this very voice borne from heaven, for we were with him on the holy mountain"—*2Peter 1:16-18*

These words of Peter are extremely noteworthy to show no one other than the Father can be YHWH. The most obvious thing seen here would be *"this is my beloved son, with whom I am well pleased"*, which is said several times in the witness of the gospels[116]. But what I see to be the more important thing said in this verse is, *"when he received honor and glory from God the Father"*. The reason this is so important is seen in Peter's testimony from Acts where he says *"Let all the house of Israel therefore know for certain that God has made him both Lord and Christ, this Jesus whom you crucified"*[117], *"God, having raised up his servant, sent him to you first, to bless you by turning every one of you from your wickedness"*[118] and *"God exalted him at his right hand as Leader and Savior, to give repentance to Israel and forgiveness of sins"*[119]. These are but a few examples, which I believe to be sufficient for my purpose.

---

[116] Matthew 3:17, 17:5, Mark 1:1, 9:7, Luke 3:22
[117] Acts 2:36
[118] Acts 3:26

Peter states that Jesus received *"honor and glory from God the Father"* and that they bore witness of the voice from heaven which said, *"This is my beloved son with whom I am well pleased"*. If, as it is supposed, God is a tripartite being, then most certainly, were a person other than the Father included, we would see Peter preach this fact. Yet that is not the case, but rather he is found proclaiming that God made Jesus both Lord and Christ, Jesus is God's servant whom He raised, and God exalted him.

Furthermore, there is no person mentioned which includes the so-called person of the Holy Spirit. The only reference to a person that is attached to God is the Father, of whom also gave Jesus glory and honor. Thus, once more it must be acknowledged there is no justification for any person other than the Father to be called God.

25. *See what kind of love the Father has given to us, that we should be called children of God; and so we are. The reason why the world does not know us is that it did not know him—1John 1:3*

A logical and sensible mind understands that only a Father can have children, thus it would reason that the Father is our God, because He is our Father and we are His children. Furthermore, John tells us that it is the Fathers love that allows us to be called the children of God, further substantiating that our Father is also our God. It is plain ignorance to suppose that we are children of a God the son, for scripture never mentions such a thing.

The apostle in the final sentence states *"the world...does not know Him (the Father)"*. I believe this to be significant due to a statement he makes in his gospel. John records these words of Jesus, *"If I glorify myself, my glory is nothing. It is my Father who glorifies me, of whom you say, 'He is our God.' But you have not known him. I know him. If I were to say that I do not know him, I would be a liar like you, but I do know him and I keep his word"*[120]. This clarifies for us that the one the world does not know, is the same person the Pharisee's claimed to be their God, namely, the Father.

Another important point is that Jesus is consistently described as the son of God. We to are said to be sons of God, as Paul writes in Romans *"For all who are led by the Spirit of God are sons of God"* and in Galatians *"for in Christ Jesus you are all sons of God, through faith"*.

In addition to this, we find in the gospel of John that Jesus is quoted as saying that we are his brothers[121]. Therefore, Jesus is our brother. This being the case, if he is God, then that would mean we are brothers of God Himself. This is admittedly absurd, yet if the claim that Jesus is God be true, so to must this idea be true.

26. *My little children, I am writing these things to you so that you may not sin. But if anyone does sin,*

---

[120] John 8:54-55
[121] John 20:17

we have an advocate with the Father, Jesus Christ the righteous. He is the propitiation for our sins, and not for ours only but also for the sins of the whole world.—1John 2:1-2

In considering the last part of this verse which speaks of the propitiation for ours and the worlds sins it, reminds me of what John says in his gospel *"for God so loved the world, that He gave his only Son, that whoever believes in him should not perish but have eternal life"*[122]. This is significant because God and His son are not the same persons, otherwise the son could not be given by God. It is extremely important to recognize that it does not say "God the Father", "God our Father", or any such thing. It simply states that God gave His son. This is verified in John chapter five verse twenty-four, *"Truly, truly, I say to you, whoever hears my word and <u>believes Him who sent me</u> has eternal life…"*, with *Him* referring no doubt to the Father, as the context would agree. In chapter seventeen verse three John fully reveals who did the sending, and the one that was sent, saying *"This is eternal life, that they believe in You (the Father he is praying to) the only true God, and Jesus Christ whom you have sent"*.

In addition, there is reference to Jesus the Messiah being our advocate with the Father, which Paul also speaks of in first Timothy writing that he is the *"mediator between God and man"* and he is *"the*

---

[122] John 3:16

man Christ Jesus".[123] It is important to notice that he is and advocate *with* the Father and is said to be a mediator *between* God and man, and that as a man. So, this clearly shows that God is one of the party's that Jesus is mediating between, thus negating the possibility of Jesus being God.

Furthermore, just as John writes of Jesus here, that being, he is the righteous one, Peter as well gives this testimony in Acts saying *"But you denied the Holy and Righteous One, and asked for a murderer to be granted to you"*.[124] The title *Righteous One* appears to be a reference to Isaiah fifty three verse eleven which reads *"by his knowledge shall the righteous one, my servant, make many to be accounted righteous, and he shall bear their iniquities"*. Verse nine is the reason he is given this title, as the prophet says *"he had done no violence, and there was no deceit in his mouth"*[125].

Another thing I believe that must be asked is, if Jesus is God, why is he an advocate with the Father? It appears that John is implying that it is the Father we are sinning against, without the mention of any other person. This fact is seen in the words of Jesus as he teaches us how to pray stating, *"Our Father in heaven…forgive us our debts (sin)"*. John makes this statement later in the chapter concerning sin, *"for all*

---

[123] 1Timothy 2:5
[124] Acts 3:13-14
[125] This seems to speak of his purity and the absence of wickedness. He was the lamb of God without spot or blemish, sinless

that is in the world-the desires of the flesh and the desires of the eyes and pride in possessions-is not from the Father but is from the world"[126] **Notice that the sinful things are said to not be of the** *Father.* **In the very next verse John writes** *"and the world is passing away along with its desires, but whoever does the will of God abides forever"*[127]. **The context here makes it clear that the Father is whose will we are to obey rather than the worldly desires.**

That leaves it to be understood that the Father is the one we sin against, and He is the one we are to seek forgiveness from, which comes through our advocate, Jesus.

Furthermore, seeing it is to be understood that God consists of multiple persons, that would mean that we must have an advocate with each party, unless it is stated that one is an advocate for himself. But we do not find anywhere in scripture the mention of another God person we need an advocate with other than the Father.

26. *Beloved, if our heart does not condemn us, we have confidence before God; and whatever we ask we receive from Him, because we keep His commandments and do what pleases Him. And this is His commandment, that we believe in the name of His Son Jesus Christ and love one another, just as He has commanded us—1John 3:21-23*

---

[126] 1 John 2:16
[127] 1 John 2:17

This passage speaks of similar things as the one mentioned just prior. The major points of emphasis are his statements *have confidence before God, we receive from Him, we keep His commandments, this is His commandment, the name of His son Jesus,* and *as he has commanded.*

The key to understanding who God is in this passage begins with *have confidence before God.* Starting from this point gives us who the *He* and *His* is referring to in the statements I just presented. Thus, we receive from God, it is His commandments, and it is His son. If then Jesus is God's son, then it would indicate that no one other than the Father is God according to this passage.

You can also refer to the notes from first John chapter two verses one and two and the text from his gospel for more explanation.

27. *In this the love of God was made manifest among us, that God sent his only Son into the world, so that we might live through him. In this is love, not that we have loved God but that he loved us and sent his Son to be the propitiation for our sins. Beloved, if God so loved us, we also ought to love one another. No one has ever seen God; if we love one another, God abides in us and his love is perfected in us. By this we know that we abide in him and he in us, because he has given us of his Spirit. And we have seen and testify that the Father has sent his Son to be the Savior of the world. Whoever confesses that Jesus is the Son of God, God abides in him, and he in God.*

So we have come to know and to believe the love that God has for us. God is love, and whoever abides in love abides in God, and God abides in him—1John 4:9-16

The opening of verse nine is almost a word for word quote from John chapter three verse sixteen. As has been presented and will continue to be so within the epistles of John, God is always associated with the Father, and that without exception.

In this passage it can be seen clearly that God and Father are used interchangeably for the same being. The most evident example of this is found in two portions from the letter, those being *"God sent His only son into the world"* and *"the Father has sent His son to be savior of the world"*. So, we can see that God and Father both refer to the same being who sent His son. If the son is God's, then he cannot also be God. John as well proclaims what is also seen in the chapter two text mentioned, which can also be referenced in connection with this.

In addition to this, the apostle also speaks of abiding in God, something very similar he also mentions in his gospel, *"I in them and you in me, that they may become perfectly one, so that the world may know that you sent me and loved them even as you loved me"*.[128]

I also want to draw attention to another interesting detail found here. Three times the son is

---

[128] John 17:23

said to be sent, with two saying God sent Him, and one saying the Father sent Him, whereas Jesus is called or alluded to as *the son of God* four times.

There is also in this passage something that causes a contradiction if indeed the son is God as well. The apostle writes that "*no one has ever seen God*". So, it would be impossible for any man to be seen as God, seeing he says, "*no one has **ever** seen God*". Why? Because God is spirit, as Jesus tells us in the gospel of John[129]. Jesus also reveals in that passage who God is, saying "*the true worshipers will worship the Father in spirit and truth*".[130] Thus, if the Father is said to be worshipped in spirit and truth, and God is to be worshiped in spirit and truth (as verse twenty-four states) in the same dialogue, one must conclude there is no other person but the Father considered to be God in Jesus's mind.

This, I would hope, is something that one with a reasonable mind will acknowledge to be consistent with what I am presenting, there is no other person contained within the title God besides the Father.

28. *And we know that the Son of God has come and has given us understanding, so that we may know him who is true; and we are in him who is true, in his Son Jesus Christ. He is the true God and eternal life—1John 5:20*

---

[129] John 4:24

[130] John 4:23

When this author tells us that the son of God has given us understanding, there is no shortage of passages that tell us what he means in this statement. John tells in his gospel *"no man hath seen God at any time; the only begotten Son, who is in the bosom of the Father, he hath declared him"*[131]. In the context of John chapter one verse eighteen, it is certain that when it reads no one hath seen God, it is not speaking of a physical seeing, though that is true as well, but rather a mental understanding of who God is and what rests at the heart of His Torah (law). We can see examples of Jesus doing this in places such as the Sermon on the Mount, where he interprets what God had declared. In him doing so we now know *"Him who is true"*, who John also says we are *in* through His son. Notice we are through Jesus Messiah, *"in Him who is true"*. John often uses such language as being *in* God or Jesus, such as *"in that day you will know that I am in my Father, and you in me, and I in you"*[132]. Furthermore, the writer says the one we are in, that is to say, *"Him who is true"* is *"the true God and eternal life"*. John affirms this in his gospel saying, *"this is eternal life, that they know you the only true God, and Jesus Christ whom you have sent"*.

29. Grace, mercy, and peace will be with us, from God the Father and from Jesus Christ the Father's Son, in truth and love. I rejoiced greatly to find some

---

[131] John 1:18 *American Standard Version*
[132] John 14:20

of your children walking in the truth, just as we were commanded by the Father—2John 1:3-4

Here in this passage, there is the same issue where *God* and *Father* are joined together with *the*. In the Greek text it reads παρὰθεοῦ πατρός, or *"from God Father"* in English. So, *the* is added by the translators, for a good reason though, to make it read fluently. This also could be translated as *"from God our Father"* as I mentioned in a previous section, making it read *"from God our Father and from Jesus Christ the Father's son"*. Seeing that God is our Father, and Jesus is the Fathers son[133], the only logical conclusion from this is that God is Jesus's Father as well.

Something else I would like to bring to the reader's attention is John's words *"walking in the truth"*.

Speaking of truth, which most definitely is speaking of God's word, John in his gospel records these words of Jesus *"Sanctify them in the truth; your word is truth"*[134]. When these words are said, Jesus is praying to the Father, which makes known that the word of God is the Fathers word. The final verse in chapter one of second John, verse four, confirms this saying *"as we were commanded by the Father"*. We see Jesus himself state that he as well did as the Father had commanded him, *"I know that his*

---

[133] John 20:17
[134] John 17:17

commandment is life eternal: the things therefore which I speak, even as the Father hath said unto me, so I speak"[135]. Jesus testifies he was given commandments from the Father just as we are. Scripture certainly says as well that Jesus gave us commandments, but notice what he says in this verse, *"as the Father hath said unto me, so I speak"* and *"He who sent me is with me. He has not left me alone, for I always do the things that are pleasing to him"*[136].[137]

Therefore, this shows that the commandments given to us by Jesus are actually given by the Father. Jesus is the one who, as the Samaritan women said, *"will tell us all things"*[138]. Never is it said that Jesus spoke of his own accord. Amongst the other points mentioned here, considering that the word of God is truthfully the Fathers words, it has to be concluded that the Father is God alone.

30. *Jude, a servant of Jesus Christ and brother of James, To those who are called, beloved in God the Father and kept for Jesus Christ—Jude 1:1*

Jude here informs us he is James's brother, of whom we are told is *"...the Lord's brother"*.[139] This gives us the liberty to apply both James's and Jude's views on this into one thought. Therefore, we can

---

[135] John 12:50
[136] John 8:29
[137] There is also John 14:24
[138] John 4:25
[139] Galatians 1:19

examine what was noted in James as part of this verse. Apart from that, once again we find the phrase *God the Father and*, showing a separation from that which follows, unless of course it were to say *and God the son*, or something equivalent to that. Furthermore, *God the Father* can be rendered as *God our Father*, though the majority of translations do not do so for whatever reason.

Another thing that must be addressed is the statement that we *"are kept for Jesus Christ"*. There ap-pears to be a disagreement among scholars about the word translated as *for* here in the ESV[140]. The King James reads *"preserved in Jesus"*, Rotherham's Emphasized Bible says, *"by Jesus Christ preserved"* and the International Standard reads *"kept safe by Jesus, the Messiah"*. Though not a scholar by far, I believe *kept by/in Jesus* is the proper translation.

In addition to this there is another translation issue which comes from the statement *"beloved in God the Father"*. Though this is a possibility, the majority of translations I have read use *loved by*, which seems to be more logical. Thus, as a whole it would properly read *"to those called, loved by God the Father and kept/preserved by/in Jesus Christ"*.

Once more, the consistency of the outcome does not vary, the Father alone is God.

---

[140] There are many translations that agree with this such as the *New English Translation, American Standard Version,* and *English Revised Version*

31. *The revelation of Jesus Christ, which God gave him to show to his servants the things that must soon take place. He made it known by sending his angel to his servant John, who bore witness to the word of God and to the testimony of Jesus Christ, even to all that he saw. Blessed is the one who reads aloud the words of this prophecy, and blessed are those who hear, and who keep what is written in it, for the time is near. John to the seven churches that are in Asia: Grace to you and peace from Him who is and who was and who is to come, and from the seven spirits who are before His throne, and from Jesus Christ the faithful witness, the firstborn of the dead, and the ruler of kings on earth. To him who loves us and has freed us from our sins by his blood and made us a kingdom, priests to his God and Father, to Him be glory and dominion forever and ever. Amen… "I am the Alpha and the Omega," says the Lord God, "who is and who was and who is to come, the Almighty—Revelation 1:1-6, 8*

There is a lot of information in this passage about the relationship Jesus has with his God and Father. At the very opening of this book it tells us that God Himself gave this revelation to Jesus, which gives a noticeable contrast between God and Jesus. That means then that it is Gods message and Jesus delivered it by his angel to give to the assemblies in Messiah. This is supported by the fact that Jesus always proclaimed he gave and did as the Father said commanded him to.

Another noteworthy point is when we find the writer saying *his (Jesus's) angel*. We know from his own words that he has angels. But does that imply he is God? I believe not, because he is now greater than the angels, thus they are his messengers as well. This is certainly shown to be true by the context of the statement that was mentioned above.

John also presents a major separating line between the two in verses four and five which says, *"grace to you and peace from Him who is and who was and who is to come, and from the seven spirits who are before His throne, and from Jesus Christ the faithful witness, the firstborn of the dead, and the ruler of kings on earth"*.

There are three distinctions here. First there is *"Him who is and who was and who is to come"*, secondly *"the seven spirits who are before His throne"*, and lastly *"Jesus Christ the faithful witness"*. In making this separation there is the Him who has a throne, and then Jesus Christ. It is quite illogical to suggest anyone other than *"Him who is and who was and who is to come"* can be sitting on the throne, because it is His throne, whereas Jesus is said to be the faithful witness who is the firstborn from the dead. There is no question then, the one who is said to be sitting on the throne is the one who gave the revelation to Jesus.

There is also found here that the writer, as all authors in the New Testament do, says Jesus died and was resurrected. But of God we find Paul saying that

God "*alone has immortality*"[141], which shows that God cannot possibly die, for He is spirit. Never is it said or implied that anyone can die and live at the same time as is suggested by those who cling to the God-man fallacy.

In the verses that follow, there is undeniable evidence that there is one person who is God alone. The first and most noticeable reads *"(he) made us a kingdom, priests to his God and Father"*. As has been shown several times, *his God and Father,* or something similar, is a very common statement made throughout the New Testament. What is more, a very similar statement is made later in Revelation, *"and they sang a new song, saying, "Worthy are you to take the scroll and to open its seals, for you were slain, and by your blood you ransomed people for God from every tribe and language and people and nation, and you have made them a kingdom and priests to our God, and they shall reign on the earth"*[142]. In this passage, instead of it being Jesus's God and Father, He is said to be the God of the twenty-four elders as well. Unless there are multiple Gods, it is clear that both the elders and Jesus have the same God, ours and Jesus's Father.

It should also be noted in these particular verses that the apostle records the words, *"you ransomed a people for God"*. Jesus, as this revelation God gave him explains that he ransomed something to God.

---

[141] 1 Timothy 6:13
[142] Revelation 5:9-10

God is always the one men are being ransomed or reconciled for. This would be an odd statement to say to someone who is himself God.[143] The idea that Jesus ransomed people to himself is never found in scripture.

Taking this into consideration with that mentioned previously, who God is seems to be clearly defined.

Another significant point are these words *""I am the Alpha and the Omega," says the Lord God, "who is and who was and who is to come, the Almighty"*. The reason this is so important to recognize, is because the phrase *"who is and who was and who is to come"* is found twice in this passage. The first mention of this, as has already been shown, refers to someone other than Jesus. That being the case, this present mention of the phrase must also be understood to refer to the one called Jesus's God. Because Jesus's God gave him the message of the Revelation, He must also be the one called *the Lord God*. There is no evidence to validate that this refers to any person other than the Father. Furthermore, it is never found in scripture that *Almighty*, or *Lord God* are claimed, or even implied, to be titles given to Jesus.

---

[143] This was said in heaven after his resurrection when he supposedly returned to the eternal glory he has always possessed

5 Jesus Teaches How to Pray

"Call no man your father on earth, for you have one Father, who is in heaven. —Matthew 23:9

In reading this verse Jesus makes it clear that our Father is in heaven. This brings a great deal of clarity when we consider that God is Jesus's Father just as He is ours. Taking this into thought, it would be impossible to have a multi-person God seeing that God is our Father and Jesus is said to be our lord, Messiah and even elder brother, but never our Father[144], which he would have to be if he is truly YHWH.

Seeing that our Father is in heaven, it leads me to my next subject, Jesus teaches us to pray to this being he calls our Father in heaven.

"And when you pray, do not heap up empty phrases as the Gentiles do, for they think that they will be heard for their many words. Do not be like them, for your Father knows what you need before you ask him. Pray then like this: "Our Father in heaven, hallowed be your name. Your kingdom come, your will be done, on earth as it is in heaven. Give us this day our daily bread, and forgive us our debts, as we also have forgiven our debtors. And lead us not into temptation, but deliver us from evil.

---

[144] And I would contest our God as well

For if you forgive others their trespasses, your heavenly Father will also forgive you, but if you do not forgive others their trespasses, neither will your Father forgive your trespasses.—Matthew 6:7-15

This gives a very important revelation when we think through this matter of God being the Father alone. Here are several relevant things the writer says.

- *When you pray...do not be like them, for your Father knows what you need before you ask him.*
- *Pray like this: "Our Father in heaven, hallowed be your name, your kingdom come, your will be done on earth as it is in heaven*
- *If you forgive...your heavenly Father will forgive*

The first thing we see is Jesus saying. *"when you pray"* and subsequently revealing to whom we are to pray to, saying *"your Father knows what you need before you ask"*. Who we are told to pray to is central, in that this is how we are instructed to pray. It is also important because that debunks prayer to any other being, and only gives the Father the ability to know beforehand. It is never found or implied in scripture that any other person or being inherently had/has foreknowledge, nor does anyone claim to have such.[145]

---

[145] In Matthew 24:36 Jesus reveals there are things he does not know

This passage also contains something related to this that is not so obvious, which is who he is telling us not to pray like. It seems quite certain when Jesus says, *"do not be like them"*, he suggests those we are not to be like are praying to the exact same person (God) as those whom he is teaching to pray. This is proven in John's gospel which says *"we were not born of sexual immorality. We have one Father-even God"* [146] which is followed by Jesus saying to them, *"If God were your Father, you would love me, for I came from God and I am here"*[147].

Later, in John chapter eight there is another significant statement by Jesus *"it is my Father who glorifies me, of whom you say, 'He is our God'"*[148]. So, in this it becomes evident that when Jesus says Father, he is referring to the God we are to pray to and the God the Pharisee's claimed to be their Father. Furthermore, John chapter twenty verse seventeen records these words of Jesus *"do not cling to me, for I have not yet ascended to the Father; but go to my brothers and say to them, 'I am ascending to my Father and your Father, to my God and your God"*.

Considering all of the evidence given here demonstrating that we are instructed to pray to the Father and no other being, He remains the only one who is God. To further establish this, here are some

---

[146] John 8:41
[147] John 8:42
[148] John 8:54

examples of Jesus's prayers on his behalf to the Father (God):

At that time Jesus declared, "I thank you, Father, Lord of heaven and earth, that you have hidden these things from the wise and understanding and revealed them to little children—Matthew 11:25 [149]

And going a little farther he fell on his face and prayed, saying, "My Father, if it be possible, let this cup pass from me; nevertheless, not as I will, but as you will." And he came to the disciples and found them sleeping. And he said to Peter, "So, could you not watch with me one hour? Watch and pray that you may not enter into temptation. The spirit indeed is willing, but the flesh is weak." Again, for the second time, he went away and prayed, "My Father, if this cannot pass unless I drink it, your will be done."

Matthew—26:39-42

- *And going a little farther, he fell on the ground and prayed that, if it were possible, the hour might pass from him. And he said, "Abba, Father, all things are possible for you. Remove this cup from me. Yet not what I will, but what you will—Mark 14:35-36*
- *In these days he went out to the mountain to pray, and all night he continued in prayer to God—Luke 6:12*[150]

---

[149] This and Luke 10:21 can both be compared to Acts 17:24-25 in relation to *"Lord of heaven and earth"*, **"The God who made"**

- *In that same hour he rejoiced in the Holy Spirit and said, "I thank you, Father, Lord of heaven and earth, that you have hidden these things from the wise and understanding and revealed them to little children; yes, Father, for such was your gracious will—Luke 10:21*
- *So they took away the stone. And Jesus lifted up his eyes and said, "Father, I thank you that you have heard me. I knew that you always hear me, but I said this on account of the people standing around, that they may believe that you sent me—John 11:41-42*
- *When Jesus had spoken these words, he lifted up his eyes to heaven, and said, "Father, the hour has come; glorify your Son that the Son may glorify you…I glorified you on earth, having accomplished the work that you gave me to do. And now, Father, glorify me in your own presence with the glory that I had with you before the world existed—John 17:1, 9*

---

[150] This verse is particularly important. In this text Jesus is said to have *"continued in prayer to God"*. If indeed Jesus himself was God as well, this would be an extremely confusing statement. The reason being, he would be praying to himself, along with the Father (and the holy spirit), seeing that each of them are considered to be God

6 Jesus Was Raised by God

Another subject I would like to bring attention to is the numerous times in scripture it is recorded that God, a singular person, raised Jesus from the dead. Though some may contest that Jesus raised himself[151], scripture does not bear this out.

That being said, I believe this is well worth mentioning in determining who the New Testament writers understood the term God (YHWH) to be applied to.

1. *This Jesus God raised up, and of that we all are witnesses. Being therefore exalted at the right hand of God, and having received from the Father the promise of the Holy Spirit, he has poured out this that you yourselves are seeing and hearing—Acts 2:32*

The opening words of this verse, *"this Jesus God raised up"*, reveals that God is a separate person from anyone else, including Jesus. This is most visibly seen by means of the writer specifically saying God raised Jesus. The fact that Jesus died[152] is

---

[151] I find this idea ridiculous though there are two references that seem to possibly suggest such, John 10:17-18; The current Orthodox definition of death is really the only thing that can even allow such a notion

[152] he ceased to have breath and consciousness; Psalms 115:17, Ecclesiastes 9:5

irrefutably proof he was a separate being from God, which is what makes his resurrection so momentous.

In addition to this, more evidence comes from the statement *this Jesus,* which is a reference to the beginning of this sermon. This is seen when Peter tells those listening *"Jesus of Nazareth, a man attested to you by God with mighty works and wonders and signs that God did through him"*[153]. These words create even more of a distinction between God and others, especially Jesus, for he tells us he is a man. In both of these statements it is the person of God who is performing these actions, as it states, He raised Jesus who was attested by God, via the works He did through him.

The message also shows that Jesus sits at the right hand of the one who raised him and who did mighty works through him. Scripture mentions numerous times this fact, instructing that after his resurrection, he did not just sit at the right hand of God, but was *exalted* to sit at His right hand. This implies it is a position he had not previously possessed. Furthermore, the Bible clearly says Jesus was exalted by God Himself, which clearly differentiates the two from one another.

The last thing I want the reader to take note of is that Jesus was also at this time said to be given something by the Father, that being the Holy Spirit. The giving of the Holy Spirit is spoken of by Jesus in

---

[153] Acts 2:22

John chapter fourteen. In the sixteenth verse he tells his disciples *"I will ask the Father, and he will give you another Helper, to be with you forever"*. He is recorded to mention this in Acts chapter one verse eight as well, which reads *"But you will receive power when the Holy Spirit has come upon you, and you will be my witnesses in Jerusalem and in all Judea and Samaria, and to the end of the earth."*. Though the texts of scripture clearly state that Jesus is said to have "poured out" the spirit, it is also written with the same clearness that the Father is the possessor of the spirit that was given to his disciples.

2. *The God of Abraham, the God of Isaac, and the God of Jacob, the God of our fathers, glorified his servant Jesus, whom you delivered over and denied in the presence of Pilate, when he had decided to release him. But you denied the Holy and Righteous One, and asked for a murderer to be granted to you, and you killed the Author of life, whom God raised from the dead. To this we are witnesses—Acts 3:13-15*

In this passage a surprising statement is made by someone who is supposedly a Trinitarian, that being, *"the God of Abraham, the God of Isaac, and the God of Jacob, the God of our fathers, glorified His servant Jesus"*. The words, just as the previous passage addressed from chapter two, are spoken by Peter. I do not think he could express any simpler the separation there is between God and all other beings than what he says here. The simple fact that Jesus is called His servant gives a clear representation of his relationship to the person of God. But this gives a fuller description of who this God is, namely *"the God of Abraham, the God of Isaac, and the God of Jacob, the God of our fathers"*.

That Jesus is the servant of the God of Israel is not something unknown to either Testaments. An example from the Old Testament is seen in Psalms chapter forty verses seven through ten which says, *"then I said, "Behold, I have come; in the scroll of the book it is written of me: I delight to do your will, O my God; your law is within my heart." I have told the glad news of deliverance in the great congregation; behold, I have not restrained my lips, as you know, O Lord. I have not hidden your deliverance within my heart; I have spoken of your faithfulness and your salvation; I have not concealed your steadfast love and your faithfulness from the great congregation"*. In the gospel of John Jesus testifies to this as well saying, *"but I do as the Father has commanded me, so that the world may know that I love the Father"*[154].

The final verse of this passage is found to report that, *the God of Abraham, the God of Isaac, the God of Jacob*, raised Jesus His servant. Jesus being raised from the dead was performed because of his faithful servant hood. This resurrection is when his glorification literally took place as Paul says, *"He

---

[154] John 14:31

worked in Christ when He raised him from the dead and seated him at His right hand in the heavenly places, far above all rule and authority and power and dominion, and above every name that is named, not only in this age but also in the one to come. And He put all things under his feet and gave him as head over all things to the church, which is his body, the fullness of him who fills all in all"[155].

Also, it needs to be pointed out that Jesus is described as, *"the author of life"*. This may be construed as him being God through applying *author* to him. That is not the case though. This is simply referring to him being the firstborn from the dead, and through that, he is the "father" of eternal life, that is to say, the beginning of eternal life through him being raised from the dead. This is described in Colossians which reads *"he is the image of the invisible God, the firstborn of all creation. For through him all things were created, in heaven and on earth, visible and invisible, whether thrones or dominions or rulers or authorities-all things were created through him and for him. And he is before all things, and in him all things hold together. And he is the head of the body, the church. He is the beginning, the firstborn from the dead, that in everything he might be preeminent"*[156].

3. *Moses said, 'The Lord God will raise up for you a prophet like me from your brothers. You shall*

---

[155] Ephesians 1:20-23
[156] Colossians 1:15-18

listen to him in whatever he tells you. And it shall be that every soul who does not listen to that prophet shall be destroyed from the people.' And all the prophets who have spoken, from Samuel and those who came after him, also proclaimed these days. You are the sons of the prophets and of the covenant that God made with your fathers, saying to Abraham, 'And in your offspring shall all the families of the earth be blessed.' God, having raised up his servant, sent him to you first, to bless you by turning every one of you from your wickedness.—Acts 3:22-26

This is one of the amazing prophecies given about the Messiah, which the Samaritan women understood, saying *"I know that Messiah is coming (he who is called Christ). When he comes, he will tell us all things"*[157]. The apostle points to the words that Moses spoke of concerning a prophet that was to come, showing from this that Jesus is the fulfillment of this prophecy. It seems the Samaritan women had a knowledge of scripture because YHWH says this of the prophet who was to come, *"I will put my words in his mouth, and he shall speak to them all that I command him"*[158], which is what the Almighty declared in Matthew *"this is my beloved Son, with whom I am well pleased; listen to him"*[159]. The words YHWH gave Moses say, *"I (YHWH) will raise up a prophet...you shall listen to him"*, display that this

---

[157] John 4:25
[158] Deuteronomy 18:18
[159] Matthew 17:5

prophet is raised up by God and that he only speaks what he is commanded to. Furthermore, the Almighty says, *"I will put my words in his mouth"*, which is very substantial because He says *My word...his mouth*. The reason for this is that he is called in Revelation *"the word of God"* and of course what is said in John chapter one. Considering that God put His word in the prophets' mouth, we must conclude that Jesus himself is not the eternal word, nor the Almighty, but rather the fulfillment of it and the vessel through which it was given by Him. In John's gospel he acknowledges this fact saying *"I have not spoken on my own authority, but the Father who sent me has himself given me a commandment-what to say and what to speak. And I know that his commandment is eternal life. What I say, therefore, I say as the Father has told me."*[160]

I want to make one last observation for the reader to consider, that being from how this passage ends and begins. It begins by him saying the *"Lord God will raise up a prophet"* and ends with *"God having raised up his servant, sent him to you first"*. One is future tense and the other is past tense with both referring to the same subject. The prophet that was to come is His servant that came, showing that from the beginning to the end the Messiah has and will always be the servant of YHWH.

4. *The God of our fathers raised Jesus, whom you killed by hanging him on a tree. God exalted him at*

---
[160] John 12:49-50

his right hand as Leader and Savior, to give repentance to Israel and forgiveness of sins—Acts 5:30-31

Just as Acts chapter three verse thirteen, Peter and John tell these leaders that *"the God of our father raised Jesus"*. This text, as well as numerous other verses, informs us that God, the God of our fathers, exalted him to sit at His right hand. In this exaltation, the result was/is Jesus is leader and savior. But it has to be remembered it says God exalted him and raised him. It cannot be emphasized enough that the apostles say, *"the God of our Fathers"*.

In first Chronicles the author records these words *"O Lord, the God of Abraham, Isaac, and Israel, our fathers, keep forever such purposes and thoughts in the hearts of your people, and direct their hearts toward you"*[161] and also in second Chronicles *"O Lord, God of our fathers, are you not God in heaven? You rule over all the kingdoms of the nations. In your hand are power and might, so that none is able to withstand you"*[162]. Ezra in his writing says *"blessed be the Lord, the God of our fathers, who put such a thing as this into the heart of the king, to beautify the house of the Lord that is in Jerusalem"*[163]. All of this indicates that Jesus is not the God of their fathers, but rather, the God of their Fathers is Jesus's God. In addition to this we are told that this exaltation is at

---

[161] 1 Chronicles *29:18*
[162] 2 Chronicles *20:6*
[163] Ezra *7:27*

Gods right hand, which is something commonly seen in scripture, such as Paul telling us in very similar words that, *"Jesus is at the right hand of the God who exalted him as that he worked in Christ when he raised him from the dead and seated him at his right hand in the heavenly places"*[164].

Understanding then that God exalted Jesus to His righthand, and the Father glorified him, the outcome can only be that the Father is the God of their fathers, and Him alone.

5. So Peter opened his mouth and said: "Truly I understand that God shows no partiality, but in every nation anyone who fears him and does what is right is acceptable to him. As for the word that he sent to Israel, preaching good news of peace through Jesus Christ (he is Lord of all), you yourselves know what happened throughout all Judea, beginning from Galilee after the baptism that John proclaimed: how God anointed Jesus of Nazareth with the Holy Spirit and with power. He went about doing good and healing all who were oppressed by the devil, for God was with him. And we are witnesses of all that he did both in the country of the Jews and in Jerusalem. They put him to death by hanging him on a tree, And we are witnesses of all that he did both in the country of the Jews and in Jerusalem. They put him to death by hanging him on a tree, but God raised him on the third day and made him to appear, not to all the people but to us who had been chosen by God as

---

[164] Ephesians 1:20

witnesses, who ate and drank with him after he rose from the dead. And he commanded us to preach to the people and to testify that he is the one appointed by God to be judge of the living and the dead—Acts 10:34-42

There could be no more convincing evidence that would put an end to even the slightest possibility that there could be any other person than the Father who is God. I want to stress this point; these words are spoken by the very people that walked with the Messiah and they must be ignored to allow any other outcome. Such as when we see Peter stating, *"God anointed Jesus of Nazareth with the Holy Spirit and with power"*. This is recorded for us by Luke at Jesus's baptism *"when the Holy Spirit descended on him in bodily form, like a dove; and a voice came from heaven, "You are my beloved Son; with you I am well pleased"*[165]. These verses bring to light that the person referred to as God by Peter is the same person as the Father according to Luke.

It can also be seen that the event in Luke chapter four verse fourteen shows what happened after the anointing of the holy spirit, *"Jesus returned in the power of the Spirit to Galilee, and a report about him went out through all the surrounding country"* as Peter testifies in verses thirty seven and thirty eight of this Acts passage *"you yourselves know what happened throughout all Judea, beginning from*

---

[165] Luke 3:22

Galilee after the baptism that John proclaimed... He went about doing good and healing all who were oppressed by the devil". But it does not stop there, the writer continues on with *"for God was with him"*. God was with him, and I have to stress this, Peter asserts that God Himself was with Jesus. This causes a big problem for the multi-person God theology. We can see our Messiah in his own words say the exact same thing, *"He who sent me is with me. He has not left me alone, for I always do the things that are pleasing to him"*[166]. Peter makes it very clear that *"he commanded us to preach to the people and to testify that he is the one appointed by God"*. These disciples say they *"ate and drank with him after he rose from the dead"* during which time *"he commanded us to preach to the people and to testify that he is the one appointed by God"*. Here not just Peter, Paul, John, James or the epistles that are written, but our lord himself tells us that *"he is the one appointed by God"*. It also is pertinent that the reader remembers this is after the resurrection.

Another key thing written here is the apostle saying, *"we are witnesses of all that he did"*. We can see the Messiah say this in John's gospel, *"you also will bear witness, because you have been with me from the beginning"*[167]. Part of this witness is the fact that God raised him, and God *made him to appear,* or allowed him to be seen. That is a powerful thing that

---

[166] John 8:29
[167] John 15:27

not only did God raise him, but without His authority Jesus would not have been seen! Through his resurrection he was given, as he said, *"all authority in heaven and earth...to be judge of the living and the dead"*.

6. *"Of this man's offspring God has brought to Israel a Savior, Jesus, as he promised...Brothers, sons of the family of Abraham, and those among you who fear God, to us has been sent the message of this salvation. For those who live in Jerusalem and their rulers, because they did not recognize him nor understand the utterances of the prophets, which are read every Sabbath, fulfilled them by condemning him. And though they found in him no guilt worthy of death, they asked Pilate to have him executed. And when they had carried out all that was written of him, they took him down from the tree and laid him in a tomb. But God raised him from the dead, and for many days he appeared to those who had come up with him from Galilee to Jerusalem, who are now his witnesses to the people. And we bring you the good news that what God promised to the fathers, this he has fulfilled to us their children by raising Jesus, as also it is written in the second Psalm, "'You are my Son, today I have begotten you.' And as for the fact that he raised him from the dead, no more to return to corruption, he has spoken in this way, "'I will give you the holy and sure blessings of David.' Therefore he says also in another psalm, "'You will not let your Holy One see corruption.' For David, after he had*

served the purpose of God in his own generation, fell asleep and was laid with his fathers and saw corruption, but he whom God raised up did not see corruption. Let it be known to you therefore, brothers, that through this man forgiveness of sins is proclaimed to you, and by him everyone who believes is freed from everything from which you could not be freed by the law of Moses—Acts 13:23, 26-39

To begin, I want to focus on the beginning and ending of this passage because they are very telling. Peter exclaims *"God has brought to Israel a Savior, Jesus, as he promised"* which is followed by the same idea several verses later saying *"let it be known to you therefore, brothers, that through this man forgiveness of sins is proclaimed to you"*. This is the gospel message as is corroborated in John's gospel, *"For God so loved the world, that he gave his only Son, that whoever believes in him should not perish but have eternal life"*[168].

During this proclamation of the good news Peter tells us *"for many days he appeared to those who had come up with him from Galilee to Jerusalem, who are now his witnesses to the people"*.

It is very important that this verse is examined and considered by the reader to have a fuller understanding of the subject in this section.

We have already been informed that *God brought a savior,* which is undeniably Jesus. And now the

---

[168] John 3:16

apostle tells those listening what they are witnesses to, that being, the savior God sent and of his resurrection. As to being a witness, it was a command given to them by the lord when he said to them, *"It is not for you to know times or seasons that the Father has fixed by his own authority. But you will receive power when the Holy Spirit has come upon you, and you will be my witnesses in Jerusalem and in all Judea and Samaria, and to the end of the earth"*[169]. Another part of the process of being his witness is *"go therefore and* [170]*make disciples of all nations...teaching them to observe all that I have commanded you"*[171]. This was not information which could be considered hearsay, they saw these things with their own eyes.

The apostle speaks to the people about what was promised in the prophets and the Torah (Old Testament) to demonstrate what they witnessed, which is that God raised him from the dead. I would think this would make the reader a bit unsettled that they did not make the assertion that this Jesus they are speaking of is God himself, if it is imperative that this is under-stood for salvation. But we do find Peter saying in reference to Jesus, *"through this man forgiveness of sins is proclaimed"*. How could this apostle who is claimed to fully know the deity of the Messiah, have the audacity to call him a man when

---

[169] Acts 1:7-8
[170] Scripture does say we are to know the only true God, Jesus defines as the Father, and the Messiah He sent, this is what is essential
[171] Matthew 28:19-20

proclaiming the gospel message to these Jews! And who is he to have the nerve to convey within the same breath that God raised him from the dead! But are these statements to be considered sacrilege? Let's determine this by answering the question Peter was asked by *this man*, which is, *who do you say I am?* How did he reply? *"Simon Peter replied, "You are the Christ, the Son of the living God"*[172], which is the exact thing he is telling those who are listening, he is the promised Messiah, the son of God.

Another important fact that is of great importance the reader should take council on is the testimony given four times in this single passage that God raised Jesus from the dead. God is understood here as a single being who did this work, Jesus is the one who it was performed for. This is not testifying that Jesus, because he is God, raised himself from the dead.

Additionally, the author tells us of another quote from scripture given by Peter, *"you are my Son, today I have begotten you"*. Though the Father said at Jesus' baptism *"You are my beloved Son; with you I am well pleased"*[173] the context of *"you are my son"* in this verse refers to the resurrection of the Messiah, which is not the same way Mark uses *"my son"*. Thus, this text gives us a definitive explanation of the relationship that Jesus has with God, namely,

---

[172] Matthew 16:16
[173] Mark 1:11

he is proven to be the son of the Almighty by means of his being raised from the dead.

That being said, this as well makes certain that the God who raised Jesus from the dead, his Father, is God alone.

7. *But the words "it was counted to him" were not written for his sake alone, but for ours also. It will be counted to us who believe in him who raised from the dead Jesus our Lord, who was delivered up for our trespasses and raised for our justification—Romans 4:24-25*

Paul writes here speaking of justification, which is obtained not only because Jesus was raised from the dead, but also believing Him who raised Jesus from the dead. He expresses this in more detail in chapter ten verse nine, *"if you confess with your mouth that Jesus is Lord and believe in your heart that God raised him from the dead, you will be saved"*. This gives a richer definition of how one is saved in comparison to chapter three verse sixteen in the gospel of John *"for God so loved the world, that he gave his only Son, that whoever believes in him should not perish but have eternal life"*.

The apostle also tells us how this was accomplished, that being *"Jesus our Lord...was delivered up for our trespasses and raised for our justification"*. Though he laid his life down, it was God's plan[174] to deliver him over to accomplish the very thing the apostle speaks of.

8. *If the Spirit of Him who raised Jesus from the dead dwells in you, He who raised Christ Jesus from the dead will also give life to your mortal bodies through His Spirit who dwells in you—Romans 8:11*

The first thing I want to point out here is how affect the way a phrase is to be understood. In the King James Version this verse reads *"but if the Spirit of Him that raised up Jesus from the dead dwell in you, He that raised up Christ from the dead shall also quicken your mortal bodies by His Spirit that dwells in you"*. If you look at this closely you will see the ESV says *"His spirit <u>who</u> dwells"*, while the King James says, *"by His spirit <u>that</u> dwells in you"*. I find it very devious that the translators of the ESV would use *who* with no justification from the context of the Greek word. The writer clearly shows that the Spirit being spoken of belongs to the *Him* that raised Jesus, hence *His Spirit*. The apostle tells us as well that Jesus was raised from the dead via this very same Spirit. Seeing we are told *the Spirit of Him* raised Jesus, I am compelled to know exactly who *Him* is.

This information can be found in Galatians chapter one as Paul says *"...God the Father, who raised him from the dead"*.[175] This being so, whenever it says *God raised*, it must be recognized to be the Father that Paul has given this glory. The idea of spirit here would logically refer to the power of the

---

[174] Every time scripture speaks of Gods will being done it always refers to it being The Fathers will
[175] Galatians 1:1

Almighty of which Paul also testifies to earlier in the letter saying *"he was declared to be the Son of God in power according to the Spirit of holiness by his resurrection from the dead, Jesus Christ our Lord"*[176] . The apostle also says concerning this *"Christ was raised from the dead by the glory of the Father"*[177], which gives even more weight to the spirit being the Most High's power and not a person[178]. This also shows that the spirit comes from the Father, or is of the Father, though it uses glory as a synonym it seems.

I think it is very important for us to remember that the belief that he was raised from the dead is only valid if we believe God raised him, a title that can be given to no one other than the Father seeing it was *"by the glory of the Father"* that he was raised.

9. *He who did not spare his own Son but gave him up for us all, how will he not also with him graciously give us all things? Who shall bring any charge against God's elect? It is God who justifies. Who is to condemn? Christ Jesus is the one who died-more than that, who was raised-who is at the right hand of God, who indeed is interceding for us.—Romans 8:32-34*

The very first word in these verses is *He*. This refers to the one who raised Jesus Christ[179] to sit at

---

[176] Romans 1:4
[177] Romans 6:4
[178] This can be seen by the use of the *spirit of Him* and *His spirit*, Thus the *spirit of God* and not God the Spirit

His right hand, that being God. It is important to notice that Paul tells us Jesus is interceding for us at the right hand of God, because he also says in first Timothy chapter two verse four, *"for there is one God, and there is one mediator between God and men, the man Christ Jesus"*. This helps to give a better understanding of who Jesus is in relation to God as he sits at His[180] right hand: he mediates and intercedes for us to God. Considering that Paul says *"how will He not also with him graciously give us all things"*, which shows the one who gave His son is the provider of these things as the apostle also writes in Philippians *"and my God will supply every need of yours according to his riches in glory in Christ Jesus"*[181].

Another important thing seen here are these words, *it is God who justifies*. There is a good description of this in First Corinthians and Paul's letter to Titus. In both of these texts the same idea is described, but it is done so a little more in-depth than Romans. They read *"and such were some of you. But you were washed, you were sanctified, you were justified in the name of the Lord Jesus Christ and by the Spirit of our God"*[182] and *"but when the goodness and loving kindness of God our Savior appeared, he saved us, not because of works done by us in*

---

[179] Paul clearly tells us Jesus was the son of the one who raised him from the dead
[180] God's
[181] Philippians 4:19
[182] 1Corinthians 6:11

righteousness, but according to his own mercy, by the washing of regeneration and renewal of the Holy Spirit, whom he poured out on us richly through Jesus Christ our Savior, so that being justified by his grace we might become heirs according to the hope of eternal life"[183]. This also brings clarity to who this God that justifies in Romans is and who He is not. There is also this statement by Paul *"He who did not spare His own Son but gave him up for us all"* which precedes *"how will He not also with him graciously give us all things"*. This idea is also applicable to Jesus for he says, *"And Jesus came and said to them, "All authority in heaven and on earth has been given to me"*[184], *"The Father loves the Son and has given all things into his hand"*[185], *"My Father, who has given them to me, is greater than all, and no one is able to snatch them out of the Father's hand"*[186], *"Jesus, knowing that the Father had given all things into his hands, and that he had come from God and was going back to God"*[187], *"For I have given them the words that you gave me, and they have received them and have come to know in truth that I came from you; and they have believed that you sent me"*[188], and *"Father, I desire that they also, whom you have given me, may be with me where I am, to see my*

---

[183] Titus 3:4
[184] Matthew 28:18
[185] John 3:35
[186] John 10:29
[187] John 13:3
[188] John 17:8

glory that you have given me because you loved me before the foundation of the world"[189].

We are also taught by Jesus to pray to the Father and ask things from him and says, *"If you then, who are evil, know how to give good gifts to your children, how much more will the heavenly Father give the Holy Spirit to those who ask him"[190]*

We can see now that the Father who gave His son is the one we pray to and is the giver of all things. Therefore, He alone is God, for we are never instructed to pray to Jesus, only in his name[191].

10. *Now God indeed raised the Lord and he will raise us by His power—1Corinthians 6:14 (NET)*

Scripture shows us when power is used in relation to God's work it refers to His spirit. Acts gives a great example of this truth saying *"but you will receive power when the Holy Spirit has come upon you"[192]*. This power is what Paul is alluding to that raised Jesus from the dead. The purpose of him saying this is to let the believers know that because Jesus was raised by the power of God, they too can be confident that they will be raised by this same power. This distinctly says the one who was raised is not God just as we are not. It should also be noted that it is *His power* that raised Jesus, which refers

---

[189] John 17:24
[190] Luke 11:13
[191] Scripture shows that Jesus (Yeshua) was given his name by the Father, John 17:11, 12
[192] Acts 1:8

back to God. As has already shown from Romans chapter six verse four, the one whom Paul devotes the title of God to and who raised Jesus from the dead is the Father.

11. *We are even found to be misrepresenting God, because we testified about God that he raised Christ, whom he did not raise if it is true that the dead are not raised—1Corinthians 15:15*

When scripture says God as it does here, and not God the Father, God our Father Etc., how do we know who the apostle wants us to understand God is when this is said? Here it does not refer to Jesus as the son of God so it would be inappropriate to say this refers to God the Father opposed to God the son. The apostle tells us if Jesus was not raised from the dead, we misrepresent God, Who we claim raised him. Clearly God is not the one who was raised; thus, the Messiah is not God. Ephesians tells us exactly who the God that raised Jesus from the dead is, *"I do not cease to give thanks for you, remembering you in my prayers, that the God of our Lord Jesus Christ, the Father of glory...according to the working of His great might that He worked in Christ when He raised him from the dead and seated him at his right hand in the heavenly places"*[193].

The apostle wants the reader to be informed that the Father of glory and the God of our lord is the one who raised Jesus from the dead. I would also like to

---

[193] Ephesians 1:16, 20

suggest that claiming someone other than the Father is God causes us to misrepresent Jesus as well as the Father seeing that we read in scripture *"(Father) Sanctify them in the truth; your word is truth"*.

The inspired word of truth is the Fathers and Him alone. So, unless the term God is used of false gods, it always is associated with the Father.

12. *Paul, an apostle-not from men nor through man, but through Jesus Christ and God the Father, who raised him from the dead—Galatians 1:1*

Rather than just saying God did so, the apostle gives an exact explanation of who raised Jesus telling the reader that God the Father is the one who accomplished this amazing feat. What the apostle says here helps those he wrote to grasp firmly who is spoken of when the details of scripture say God raised the Messiah. Because of this we are allowed the liberty to insert *the Father,* or even *our Father* when only the term God is used because this clearly describes who the New Testament writers say raised Jesus.

Furthermore, the apostle makes it clear that it was *"Jesus Christ and God the Father who raised him from the dead"* that gave him his apostleship. Thus, there is no one associated with the title God other than the one who raised Jesus from the dead, that being the Father, once more confirming that God is not even remotely connected to any other being in scripture.

13. *"that the God of our Lord Jesus Christ, the Father of glory, may give you a spirit of wisdom and of revelation in the knowledge of Him, having the eyes of your hearts enlightened, that you may know what is the hope to which He has called you, what are the riches of His glorious inheritance in the saints, and what is the immeasurable greatness of His power toward us who believe, according to the working of His great might that He worked in Christ when He raised him from the dead and seated him at His right hand in the heavenly places, far above all rule and authority and power and dominion, and above every name that is named, not only in this age but also in the one to come"—Ephesians 1:17-21*

Many people have told me that I twist scripture to fit my doctrine. I unashamedly reject that accusation because I merely say what I find to be the revelation of scripture, and most times without any explanation needed other than the words written to support my position. When saying the Father is the only one who is God, I only need to bring the reader's attention to passages such as this one from Ephesians which begins by saying *"the God of our lord Jesus Christ, the Father of glory"*.

The first thing that jumps off of the page is quite ironic considering my purpose for writing this book, that being Paul wishes that the God of our lord Jesus Christ *"may give you a spirit of wisdom and of revelation in the knowledge of Him"*. The irony is obvious, Paul wants us to have a spirit of wisdom and revelation in the knowledge of the God of Jesus Christ. How exactly this can be construed to mean anything other than what it says should confuse the logical mind.

The apostle continues exhorting us to remember that the God of our lord called us. Paul also desired that we know the riches of His glorious inheritance in the saints, the immeasurable greatness of His power toward believers, that He raised Jesus and that He seated Jesus at His right hand in the heavenly places. The writer also informs us why and how Jesus has the authority he has as he ends the text, that being because his God *"seated him at His right hand in the heavenly places, far above all rule and authority and power and dominion, and above every name that is named"*.

The main point though is demonstrating who it was that raised Jesus from the dead, who without question has been shown to be his God whom the apostle gives this honor to, He is *the Father of glory.*

14. *In him also you were circumcised with a circumcision made without hands, by putting off the body of the flesh, by the circumcision of Christ, having been buried with him in baptism, in which you were also raised with him through faith in the powerful working of God, who raised him from the dead—Colossians 2:12*

Though this is speaking of us having been given a new life through the resurrection of Christ, it does address the subject I am focusing on in this chapter, which is that God raised Jesus.

Once again the apostle speaks of the power of God being connected with the resurrection, which has already been explained as signifying the Spirit of God as Paul writes in Romans *"may the God of hope fill you with all joy and peace in believing, so that by the power of the Holy Spirit you may abound in hope"*[194].

To make it brief God raised Jesus by His power, showing two persons, one being the God who raised and the second Jesus who was raised, thus, one person who is God, which has been abundantly shown to be the Father.

15. *How you turned to God from idols to serve the living and true God...to wait for His Son from heaven, whom He raised from the dead, Jesus who delivers us from the wrath to come—1Thessalonians 1:9b-10*

This opening statement *"the living and true God"* is very similar to what Jesus says in John chapter seventeen verse three designating the Father as being *"the only true God"*. With that in mind, there is an interesting combination of persons mentioned here. They include: idols, the living and true God, and Jesus. The first two are obviously contrary to each other because you must turn from one to serve the other. And as we are told, the Thessalonians turned

---

[194] Romans 15:13

from serving these false gods to serve the living and true God.

That which I find interesting comes when Jesus is introduced into the picture. If indeed the Father isn't the only one who is God as some suppose, this would make Jesus the very thing they have turned away from, an idol. This is so because Jesus was raised by the living and true God.

If indeed Jesus was dead, according to the Biblical definition, and the living God was not, one can only come to the conclusion that the Father who raised the son is only possible person qualified to be the living and true God. This is in agreement with John seven-teen as I previously mentioned, which says *"know you (Father), the only true God"*.

16. For since we believe that Jesus died and rose again, even so, through Jesus, God will bring with him those who have fallen asleep—1Thessalonians 4:14

I want to open by pointing back to the first chapter of this epistle. Starting with verse two we see that Paul writes *"We give thanks to God always for all of you"* and in verse three *"remembering before our God and Father your work of faith and labor of love and steadfastness of hope in our Lord Jesus Christ"*. This establishes a good foundation to determine who the apostle identifies as *God* which is *our Father*.

With that said, there can be no mistake, *the living and true God* mentioned in chapter one verse nine b is *our God and Father* whom they *give thanks to always* and is the one who raised Jesus from the dead.

17. *Now may the God of peace who brought again from the dead our Lord Jesus, the great shepherd of the sheep, by the blood of the eternal covenant, equip you with everything good that you may do His will, working in us that which is pleasing in His sight, through Jesus Christ, to whom be glory forever and ever. Amen—Hebrews 13:20-21*

The opening verse says a great deal about the issue of more than one person being God. The apostle begins with *"the God of peace"*[195], whom he writes is the one *"who brought again from the dead our lord Jesus"*. Though obviously we see that God raised Jesus, there is something I think may be overlooked by most.

In referring to whom *the God of peace* raised from the dead, we are told it was <u>our</u> *Lord Jesus*. I want to emphasize the word *our* because without question it describes them to be two completely separate persons. Thus, you have *the God of peace* and *our Lord*, showing *our Lord* cannot be *the God of peace* seeing *the God of peace* raised him up. Taking this into account, it must be that *His* always refers to

---

[195] This phrase is mentioned four other times: Romans 15:33, 16:20, Philippians 4:9, 1 Thessalonians 5:23

the God of peace in this passage just as *"to whom be glory forever and ever"*[196].

Speaking of Jesus, we are told he is *the great shepherd,*[197] of which Jesus often says of himself, and that these things are done *through Jesus Christ,* again showing *the God of peace* is a separate person.

18. *Blessed be the God and Father of our Lord Jesus Christ! According to His great mercy, He has caused us to be born again to a living hope through the resurrection of Jesus Christ from the dead— 1Peter 1:3*

Time and again we read the words *"blessed be the God and Father of our lord"*. Many say, "This speaks of Jesus's humanity and does not mean he isn't God", but there is a problem with that logic. We are told here that the God and Father of Jesus is the one who *caused us to be born again…according to His great mercy*. This great mercy is given to us through the resurrection of Jesus Christ from the dead which has already been shown to be the work of the Father as well. Looking at his mention of *"a living hope"*, which exists because Jesus was raised from the dead, we can find this mentioned in Titus chapter three verses four through seven as well, *"but when*

---

[196] This phrase is mentioned four other times and is always said of the Father. Galatians 1:5, Philippians 4:20, 1 Timothy 1:17, 2 Timothy 4:18

[197] This was prophesied about him in the prophet Micah *"And you, O Bethlehem, in the land of Judah, are by no means least among the rulers of Judah; for from you shall come a ruler who will shepherd my people Israel"*-Micah 5:2

the goodness and loving kindness of God our Savior appeared, He saved us, not because of works done by us in righteousness, but according to His own mercy, by the washing of regeneration and renewal of the Holy Spirit, whom He poured out on us richly through Jesus Christ our Savior, so that being justified by His grace we might become heirs according to the hope of eternal life". In this passage from Titus there is now the liberty to use the phrased *"the God and Father of our Lord Jesus Christ"* interchangeably with *God our Savior*[198].

Yet again we are left with the same conclusion, the Father is God alone.

19. *He was foreknown before the foundation of the world but was made manifest in the last times for the sake of you who through him are believers in God, who raised him from the dead and gave him glory, so that your faith and hope are in God—1Peter 1:20-21*

Though this is a little off topic, I see in the opening words of these verses, *""he was foreknown before the foundation of the world but was made manifest in the last times for the sake of you",* how Johns words *"the word was with God"* is to be understood. The Messiah, who was made flesh, was foreknown before the foundation of the world. This is

---

[198] This title is also written in Luke chapter one when Mary praised the Almighty for what he promised. This is important because it shows she had no impression of the possibility that she would be carrying YHWH in her womb

the light that brings one to the life promised in the word of the Almighty. It never says the light is the word, but rather in the word was life. It also gives clarity to what Jesus meant when saying *"before Abraham was I am (he)"* and *"Father, glorify me in your own presence with the glory that I had with you before the world existed"*. All of these things were because he was foreknown.

This same idea of *before the foundation of the world* is also included in John chapter seventeen verse twenty-four, *"Father, I desire that they...see my glory that you have given me because you loved me before the foundation of the world"*.

In addition to this, who does the apostle say foreknew the messiah's coming? There is but one answer, the God who raised Jesus from the dead, which according to verses two and three is the Father.

The ultimate goal according to the writer is that our *"faith and hope are in God"*.

7 Jesus Given Authority by God

The scripture consistently communicates to us that Jesus was given the authority that he had, it was not inherent, as it would be had he been God. He and the other New Testament writers expressed openly that the Father gave this authority to him. So, I am going to go through the verses and passages where we find this is illustrated as more evidence that only the Father is God and no other.

1. *But that you may know that the Son of Man has authority on earth to forgive sins"-he then said to the paralytic-"Rise, pick up your bed and go home." And he rose and went home. When the crowds saw it, they were afraid, and they glorified God, who had given such authority to men—Matthew 9:6-8*

There are two important things found in this passage. Firstly, Jesus says he has authority on *earth* to forgive sins. It does not say "that you may know I have authority to forgive sins in heaven and earth, which many would suggest this implies. Interestingly we find Jesus also gave this authority to his disciples as recorded in John's gospel, *if you forgive the sins of any, they are forgiven them; if you withhold forgiveness from any, it is withheld".*[199] Thus, this

---

[199] John 20:23

indicates that it was something he acquired from his Father because it was only on earth that he had authority to do so[200]. This is also seen through the last section of verse eight, *they glorified God, who had given such authority to men.* Though these Jews, as it says, were afraid, they did not seem adhere to a belief that God alone can forgive sins in the way Jesus did. This is shown because they saw this authority was given to a man. The significance of this last part is that they glorified God because this authority was given to a man. Obviously, they did not see Jesus to be God because of this, but instead glorified God because of it.

2. *And Jesus came and said to them, "All authority in heaven and on earth has been given to me—Matthew 28:18*

This is a well-known, and often quoted verse. It seems though that most ignore what it says, the authority was given to him. This would logically mean he had no authority before it was given. In first Corinthians Paul gives us the same insight but with a little more detail, *"he must reign until he has put all his enemies under his feet. The last enemy to be destroyed is death. For "God has put all things in subjection under his feet." But when it says, "all things are put in subjection," it is plain that he is excepted who put all things in subjection under him. When all things are subjected to him, then the Son*

---

[200] Jesus always says the Father is in heaven and all he does is directed by Him

himself will also be subjected to him who put all things in subjection under him, that God may be all in all".[201]

Now that we have this information concerning the authority given to Jesus, the reader can see it was only given temporarily, with the end result of the one who gave the authority to be *all in all.*

Furthermore, we discover who it is that gave him authority from Paul saying, *"God has put all things in subjection under his feet".* Prior to this statement we are told who the title God is referring to *"then comes the end, when he delivers the kingdom to God the Father after destroying every rule and every authority and power".* [202] Thus, we find that after his resurrection that the Father (who is God alone) gave him the authority he possessed.

3. In that same hour he rejoiced in the Holy Spirit and said, "I thank you, Father, Lord of heaven and earth, that you have hidden these things from the wise and understanding and revealed them to little children; yes, Father, for such was your gracious will. All things have been handed over to me by my Father, and no one knows who the Son is except the Father, or who the Father is except the Son and anyone to whom the Son chooses to reveal him—Luke 10:21-22

---

[201] 1 Corinthians 15:25-28
[202] 1 Corinthians 15:24

This is another verse that the information from first Corinthians can be applied to. When the authority given to the messiah is spoken of in the Biblical writings it always agrees with what Jesus says here *"All things have been handed over to me by my Father"*, teaching us that the authority he possesses is not inherent, it is given to him. This is one of the many things the messiah says when speaking of his Father that are perplexing if one supports the notion that he is God himself.

Additionally, in this same passage we find Jesus call the Father *"Lord of heaven and earth"*. Jesus applies this title solely to the Father, because it would be ridiculous to suggest that there are three or two that are *"Lord of heaven and earth"*. If we are to accept this, the authenticity of God being referred to as ours and Jesus's Father is a falsehood because he himself is God.

Furthermore, the messiah tells those listening that the Father is the person that revealed His will, which would logically mean that no other being can be included as possessing the Fathers will. In the gospel of John Jesus tells his disciples *"whoever does not love me does not keep my words. And the word that you hear is not mine but the Fathers who sent me"*[203] and later in chapter seventeen verse eight *"For I have given them the words that you gave me, and they have received them and have come to know in truth*

---

[203] John 14:24

that I came from you; and they have believed that you sent me" and seventeen *"Sanctify them in the truth; your word is truth"*.

These are further evidence that Jesus understood very well whose purpose he was performing.

We also find in Paul's writings some insight as to what was hidden according to His will, *"In him we have redemption through his blood, the forgiveness of our trespasses, according to the riches of his grace, which he lavished upon us, in all wisdom and insight making known to us the mystery of His will, according to His purpose, which He set forth in Christ as a plan for the fullness of time, to unite all things in him, things in heaven and things on earth"*.[204] The *He* Paul is speaking of is seen in verse three of this chapter, *"Blessed be the God and Father of our Lord Jesus Christ"*.

Once again, we find the Father to be the God of heaven and earth, and Him alone.

4. *For he whom God has sent utters the words of God, for He gives the Spirit without measure. The Father loves the Son and has given all things into his hand—John 3:34-35*

John the Baptist makes a statement here that is hard to avoid although that is usually the outcome when someone is attempting to claim God consists of more than one person. We have seen already that

---

[204] Ephesians 1:7-10

Jesus was anointed by God, but now John says the Father is the being who gave the Spirit without measure to the son! To think God would in any way need to have His own power given to Him is laughable. This also demonstrates once more that the words spoken by the messiah were given to him by the Father, something that would allow him to be given the title *the word of God*. The Messiah also proclaims that the disciples who followed him belonged to the Fathers, *"Father, I desire that they also, whom you have given me, may be with me where I am, to see my glory that you have given me because you loved me before the foundation of the world"*.[205] Even his name was given to him *"I am no longer in the world, but they are in the world, and I am coming to you. Holy Father, keep them in your name, which you have given me, that they may be one, even as we are one. While I was with them, I kept them in your name, which you have given me"*.[206] Scripture time and again tells us that the Father is the possessor, and He is the giver and does so as He wills.

5. *For as the Father has life in himself, so he has granted the Son also to have life in himself. And he has given him authority to execute judgment, because he is the Son of Man—John 5:26-27*

Jesus makes it very clear here that he only has life, the ability to raise the dead[207], because it was

---

[205] John 17:24
[206] John 17:11-12

given to him. This was not an "essence" of God he possessed because of this selfsame reason. In chapter six verse forty Jesus says to those listening *"for this is the will of my Father, that everyone who looks on the Son and believes in him should have eternal life, and I will raise him up on the last day."*, explaining why he was given life within himself, it was the will of his Father Whose intent was that those who believe will be resurrected. Following verse twenty-six of chapter five there is the mention once more about the Father giving him another responsibility, judgment. He did say he was not sent to judge in his first coming, but when the second resurrection spoken of in Revelation occurs he will assume this duty as Peter says *"...he (Jesus) is the one appointed by God to be judge of the living and the dead"*.[208] Paul also speaks of this *"For to this end Christ died and lived again, that he might be Lord both of the dead and of the living"*[209] using lord instead of judge, though both refer to the same event. The union of the two is seen in second Timothy chapter four verse one *"I charge you in the presence of God and of Christ Jesus, who is to judge the living and the dead, and by his appearing and his kingdom"*.

There are two judgments that take place though, one for those who are disciples and who truly love the Almighty, of which Paul says *"Henceforth there*

---

[207] This is probably speaking of the resurrection coming because of him and not by him

[208] Acts 10:42

[209] Romans 14:9

is laid up for me the crown of righteousness, which the Lord, the righteous judge, will award to me on that Day, and not only to me but also to all who have loved his appearing"[210] and then that of the wicked as Jesus explains in Matthew chapter thirteen verses forty-nine through fifty, *so it will be at the close of the age. The angels will come out and separate the evil from the righteous and throw them into the fiery furnace. In that place there will be weeping and gnashing of teeth.*

First Corinthians gives some other details pertaining to this, which I have previously dug into. The gospel also gives another detail about the judgment he will lay down, *"if I do judge, my judgment is true, for it is not I alone who judge, but I and the Father who sent me".*[211] This reveals the judgment of the Messiah will be the judgment of the Father, he said and does everything according to the Fathers will as was shown from verse forty of chapter six.

6. *So Jesus answered them, "My teaching is not mine, but his who sent me. If anyone's will is to do God's will, he will know whether the teaching is from God or whether I am speaking on my own authority. The one who speaks on his own authority seeks his own glory; but the one who seeks the glory of him who sent him is true, and in him there is no falsehood—John 7:16-18*

---

[210] 2 Timothy 4:8
[211] 1 Corinthians 8:16

There are many verses that to some extent correspond to the fact that what he taught was not his. In order to substantiate this, here are some examples: *"Whoever does not love me does not keep my words. And the word that you hear is not mine but the Fathers who sent me"*[212] and *"I have given them your word, and the world has hated them because they are not of the world, just as I am not of the world... Sanctify them in the truth; your word is truth"*.[213] Jesus adds to this fact that if someone seeks to do Gods will, *he will know whether the teaching is from God.*

Going back to John chapter six verse forty, the gospel shows the will of God he is referring to in this passage is more forthright expressing it to be the Fathers will. Moreover, Jesus speaks of his strong desire to submit to this will spoken of, saying this, *"My food is to do the will of him who sent me and to accomplish his work"*.[214]

In Mark chapter three verse thirty-five he tells us who we are to him if we do the Fathers will, *"For whoever does the will of God, he is my brother and sister and mother."*

Therefore, with all of this said, the Father is the one possessing this will, of which Jesus is performing.

---

[212] John 14:24
[213] John 17:14, 17
[214] John 4:34

7. So Jesus said to them, "When you have lifted up the Son of Man, then you will know that I am he, and that I do nothing on my own authority, but speak just as the Father taught me. And he who sent me is with me. He has not left me alone, for I always do the things that are pleasing to him—John 8:28-29

The first thing that has to be understood in this quotation is, who is *he*? Jesus tells those listening to him, *"when you have lifted up the Son of Man, then you will know that I am (he)"*. The ending of this statement is the exact wording in the Greek of one of the Trinitarians most beloved proof text when he says, *"...before Abraham was, I am."* As I just said, what Jesus says here in John chapter eight reads just as verse fifty in the Greek text saying, *I am*. For whatever reason they decided to add *he* to verse twenty eight and not verse fifty. It makes perfect sense to say *know that I am (he)* in the context of verse twenty-eight which no one seems to argue against. So, is he saying what the Almighty says in Exodus? That is as far as one could get from what he was telling these people.

In verse twenty-five the question of these leaders and the answer of Jesus help make sense of this, *"So they said to him, "Who are you?" Jesus said to them, "Just what I have been telling you from the beginning."* This is the basis of what the Jesus says from here to the end of the chapter, telling them who he is.

In chapter seven these leaders make it frankly known how they feel about him, *"Have you also been deceived? Have any of the authorities or the Pharisees believed in him?"*[215] making it clear that when asking him who he was they definitely knew who he was said to be. Their purpose for all of the questions they ask is to catch him in something that can be used to condemn him as you can see in a discussion between Jesus and these leaders of the Jews, *"so they watched him and sent spies, who pretended to be sincere, that they might catch him in something he said, so as to deliver him up to the authority and jurisdiction of the governor. So they asked him, "Teacher, we know that you speak and teach rightly, and show no partiality, but truly teach the way of God. Is it lawful for us to give tribute to Caesar, or not?" But he perceived their craftiness, and said to them, "Show me a denarius. Whose likeness and inscription does it have?" They said, "Caesar's." He said to them, "Then render to Caesar the things that are Caesar's, and to God the things that are God's." And they were not able in the presence of the people to catch him in what he said, but marveling at his answer they became silent".*[216] So, the assumption they attempted to stone him because he "claimed to be God" is a gross misinterpretation and is totally out of the context of the debate. Who then is he saying he is?

---

[215] John 7:47-48
[216] Luke 20:20-26

Chapter four of John's gospel gives the answer, *"The woman said to him, "I know that Messiah is coming (he who is called Christ). When he comes, he will tell us all things... Jesus said to her, "I who speak to you am he".*[217] When these leaders had him arrested, illegally at that, they tried to find any reason they could to condemn him with this very thing being their reason, *"the high priest said to him, "I adjure you by the living God, tell us if you are the Christ, the Son of God." Jesus said to him, "You have said so. But I tell you, from now on you will see the Son of Man seated at the right hand of Power and coming on the clouds of heaven." Then the high priest tore his robes and said, "He has uttered blasphemy. What further witnesses do we need? You have now heard his blasphemy".*[218] Here is the charge they presented to Pilate *"And they began to accuse him, saying, "We found this man misleading our nation and forbidding us to give tribute to Caesar, and saying that he himself is Christ, a king".*[219] With this said there can be no doubt about what he intended to be understood, he is the messiah promised in the scripture.

Following Jesus's declaring that he was the messiah, he says to these people he that did nothing on his own authority, but only spoke as the Father taught him.

---

[217] John 4:25-26
[218] Matthew 26:63-65
[219] Luke 23:2

The scripture is replete, Old Testament and New Testament, with references to the obedience of the Messiah. This statement ends with *"he who sent me is with me"*. The apostle Peter says this in Acts chapter ten verse thirty-eight, *"how God anointed Jesus of Nazareth with the Holy Spirit and with power. He went about doing good and healing all who were oppressed by the devil, for God was with him."* From what Peter says here, we find that the *He* spoken of by the messiah is God, the God who is his Father and whom he always sought to please by obedience.

8. For I have not spoken on my own authority, but the Father who sent me has himself given me a commandment-what to say and what to speak. And I know that his commandment is eternal life. What I say, therefore, I say as the Father has told me—John 12:49-50

As has been shown again and again when Jesus says *Father*, he is speaking of his God. Furthermore, just as the previous verse said, he once again states that everything he said was what he was commanded by his Father to say and even tells those listening that his *Fathers* commandment is eternal life. This is very vital because he is saying that it is his Fathers words, which is the commandment given to Jesus, that is the source of eternal life.

We can find John alluding to this fact in chapter one saying *"No one has ever seen God; the only God, who is at the Father's side, he has made him known"*.[220]

The idea of no one seeing God can be understood to mean no one has fully perceived who God is and what His teachings mean, but the son made these things known through what he instructed his disciples and how he lived his life[221]. Jesus proclaims about what he taught in chapter eight *"Whoever is of God hears the words of God (what he was teaching). The reason why you do not hear them is that you are not of God."*[222] And John the Baptist said of him *"he whom God has sent utters the words of God, for he gives the Spirit without measure. The Father loves the Son and has given all things into his hand. Whoever believes in the Son has eternal life; whoever does not obey the Son shall not see life, but the wrath of God remains on him"*.[223] It should be understood that when Jesus says *whosever believes in the son* he is speaking of the words which he was commanded to say as was said by the Father *"This is my beloved Son, with whom I am well pleased; listen to him."* Therefore, just as Peter, we also should say *"Lord, to whom shall we go? You have the words of eternal life (the words God, our Father, told you to speak)"*[224].

9. *Jesus, knowing that the Father had given all things into his hands, and that he had come from God and was going back to God, rose from supper. He*

---

[220] John **1:18**
[221] It is certainly true that no man has seen God as Paul says in 1 Timothy 6:16
[222] John 8: 47
[223] John 1:32-36
[224] John 6:68

laid aside his outer garments, and taking a towel, tied it around his waist—John 13:3-4

These two verses are another witness testifying that whether authority, power, or even what he said, they were acquired by Jesus from his Father. I want to first point out in this passage that the translators add *back* in the phrase *going back to God*. In doing this they have altered the meaning of what the writer wants us to understand. To start off with the explanation for this error, the idea of him coming from God should properly be understood to mean that he was sent by God as can be seen in chapter seven verses twenty-eight and twenty-nine, *"...I have not come of my own accord. He who sent me is true, and him you do not know. I know him, for I come from him, and he sent me."* What the people say in verse twenty-six of chapter seven, *"...Can it be that the authorities really know that this is the Christ?"* gives us more insight as to exactly what the writer means by using *come from God* or even *come from heaven* as he says in another place.

In chapter sixteen the disciples say to Jesus, *"Now we know that you know all things and do not need anyone to question you; this is why we believe that you came from God."* I don't find any evidence that these men and women saw Jesus as God, but rather said he came from God[225]. The idea that any

---

[225] The idea that he *came* from God makes it very difficult to substantiate God is a *He* as scripture clearly reveals. As I have said previously, God has now become an *it* or at the least *we*

competent scholar or bible student would claim that the Jewish people expected God to descend from heaven to become a man and be their messiah is preposterous. Seeing that *back* is an addition by the translators, it should read *"going to God"*.

It wasn't that he was *going back*, but rather he was *going to* where he was destined to be according to prophecy[226]. But, if as is suggest, he is *going back* to God, who or what exactly does the word God represent if indeed God consists of multiple persons? If we are to understand God consists of more than one person, then *He* has now become an *it* that Jesus was returning to. But Jesus does not allow this interpretation saying in chapter four of John's gospel, *"...the hour is coming when neither on this mountain nor in Jerusalem will you worship the Father... true worshipers will worship the Father in spirit and truth, for the Father is seeking such people to worship him. God is spirit, and those who worship him must worship in spirit and truth".*[227]

So then, the reader must now determine themselves, is God and *it* or a *He* and did part of *it* leave and then go back to *it*?

Whatever conclusion one comes to, there can be no argument that he was given all things by the Father who is his God.

---

[226] Acts 2:34-35
[227] John 4:21, 23-24

10. *Do you not believe that I am in the Father and the Father is in me? The words that I say to you I do not speak on my own authority, but the Father who dwells in me does His works—John 14:10*

Outside of the fact that the messiah says once again what he did or said was not by his own authority, he says the Father dwells in him.

In looking at Johns gospel there are many things he says that are misunderstood, such as the opening of chapter one. How do I know this? What he says in this verse. How exactly can the Father dwell in him and him in the Father if indeed the Father is in heaven? This seems to be referring to his relationship with the Father as chapter eight verse twenty-nine states, *"And he who sent me is with me. He has not left me alone, for I always do the things that are pleasing to him."* Peter's sermon in chapter ten of Acts affirms this saying *"God was with him"*.

Furthermore, we find that this *"dwelling with in"* is not limited to just Jesus and the Father. because John also records Jesus saying, *"I in them and you in me, that they may become perfectly one, so that the world may know that you sent me and loved them even as you loved me"*.[228] Clearly this is not telling us we are equal with Jesus in his essence if indeed he is God, otherwise we to are God. The explanation is given, that they may be perfectly one, which can also be seen in verses twenty-two and twenty-three. This

---

[228] John 17:23

makes it obvious then that this refers to a perfect oneness in purpose, which is why he says he *always* does what he is told.

To make this even more certain he tells us it is the Father's works he is accomplishing, not his own. The idea here is that the Fathers word[229] is in him and that is exactly what he does, and as Peter says about the works, *"God anointed Jesus of Nazareth with the Holy Spirit and with power He went about doing good and healing all who were oppressed by the devil".*[230]

11. *When Jesus had spoken these words, he lifted up his eyes to heaven, and said, "Father, the hour has come; glorify your Son that the Son may glorify you, since you have given him authority over all flesh, to give eternal life to all whom you have given him—John 17:1-2*

The very first words we find here are informative, *"he lifted up his eyes to heaven"*. In Matthew chapter eleven verse twenty-five and Luke chapter ten verse twenty-one Jesus says, *"I thank you, Father, Lord of heaven and earth…"*, which defines who the Father in heaven he is here praying to.

Another fascinating thing to note is the writer says that Jesus asks the Father to glorify him, which seems necessary before he is able to glorify the Father. So, it's obvious the glory is given to him.

---

[229] John 17:14-17
[230] Acts 10:38

When it speaks of glory the idea is not some majestic bright lights shining that no man can see, but is speaking of him being honored, or esteemed worthy of honor for his obedience to the Father. And when this is done the Father will in turn be honored and praised for raising him from the dead, which is what this is referring to. Two times the messiah says he was given something, authority over all flesh and to give eternal life to all the Father gave him. This logically means this authority to give eternal life was not intrinsically his.

One last point I want bring to light, it is fascinating that the verse following this has him saying that the Father is *"the only true God"*.

12. *He said to them, "It is not for you to know times or seasons that the Father has fixed by his own authority—Acts 1:7*

The thing I want to focus on in this verse is Jesus' answer from stating that *"the Father has fixed by his own authority."*

To dig into why Jesus says by the Fathers authority, I am going to move on to chapter two where Peter tells those who saw the disciples filled with the Holy Spirit what allowed it to happen *"...Being therefore exalted at the right hand of God, and having received from the Father the promise of the Holy Spirit, he has poured out this that you yourselves are seeing and hearing."* Two things I want to point out, he is exalted at the right hand of

God, and he received the Holy Spirit from the Father to give his disciples.

Jesus being exalted to the right hand of God is said thirteen times in the New Testament and most of them are related to God raising him from the dead, of which is found sixteen times speaking these exact words, *"God raised from the dead"*. Paul describes what he was exalted to *"Therefore God has highly exalted him and bestowed on him the name that is above every name, so that at the name of Jesus every knee should bow, in heaven and on earth and under the earth, and every tongue confess that Jesus Christ is Lord, to the glory of God the Father"*.[231]

All throughout the gospels, as I have pointed out, what he did was not done by his authority, but rather authority only the Father possessed. He was made to be both lord and messiah. I also want the reader to notice when he says, *"it is not for you to know times or seasons"* of which he himself said he didn't know in Mark chapter thirteen verse thirty-two, *"But concerning that day or that hour, no one knows, not even the angels in heaven, nor the Son, but only the Father."* This again refers to authority, authority to decide what is and is not known by Jesus or ourselves according to His prerogative.

To top all of this off, chapter two verse twenty-two says this of Jesus *"Jesus of Nazareth, a man attested to you by God with mighty works and*

---

[231] Philippians 2:9-11

wonders and signs that God did through him", which again shows all he did was according to God's authority, along with the fact that he is a man.

We must conclude then that unless God is an *it* called *He*, the Father is God alone.

13. *Afterwards, the end—whensoever he delivereth up the kingdom unto his God and Father, whensoever he shall bring to nought all rule and all authority and power; For he must needs reign, until he shall put all his enemies under his feet: As a last enemy, death, is to be destroyed; For—He put, all things, in subjection under his feet. But, whensoever it shall be said—all things are in subjection!—it is evident that it means,—Except him who did put into subjection, unto him, the all things— But whensoever have been put into subjection, unto him, the all things, then, the Son himself, [also] shall be put in subjection unto him who put in subjection, unto him, the all things,—that, God, may be, all things in all— 1Corinthians 15:24-28 (Rotherham's Emphasized Bible)*[232]

As I have done several times to this point, I would like to once more underscore the differences in the translations. I want to start with comparing Rother-hams version, which I have used here, to most new translations. The verse I want to focus on, verse four-teen, is for the most part rendered the same as the English Standard Version which says, *"Then*

---

[232] KJV reads *"God, even the Father"* in the opening of verse 24

comes the end, when he delivers the kingdom to God the Father". The difference is somewhat subtle but very significant. In Rotherham's translation that reads, *"his God and Father"*, he gives a very clear picture of who subjects all things to the son and whom the God that will be all and all is. So then, it should be given to us as *"his God and Father"* as opposed to *"God the Father"*. The kingdom which Paul informs the reader that will be handed over is referring to the kingdom of God, or kingdom of Heaven that Jesus spoke of so often.[233] The idea of him delivering the kingdom gives the picture that it was never his but was something he was entrusted with for a period of time. It can even go as deep as to say surrendered the kingdom, which fits very well with him being subjected.

The passage also points out Jesus will only reign for a time period which ends when all things are subject to him. When the apostle refers to subjection there is one who is subjecting others to another. The one who is subjecting is the God or the messiah.

Something else interesting I want to point out is that death is spoken of as an enemy of the messiah as well as the one who subjected everything to him. This last enemy is put under his foot when death and hell are cast into the lake of fire.[234] It is so easy to see how the apostles and gospels coincide with one another. Jesus says this exact thing in a condensed

---

[233] this is actually the whole gospel, the gospel of the kingdom
[234] Revelation 20:14

form in Matthew *"All authority in heaven and on earth has been given to me"*.[235]

Something else to think about is what this passage implies, unless the Father subjected these things under Jesus, they would never be. In the end of all of this the purpose is that his God and Father may be all in all.

14. *I do not cease to give thanks for you, remembering you in my prayers, that the God of our Lord Jesus Christ, the Father of glory, may give you a spirit of wisdom and of revelation in the knowledge of Him, having the eyes of your hearts enlightened, that you may know what is the hope to which He has called you, what are the riches of His glorious inheritance in the saints, and what is the immeasurable greatness of His power toward us who believe, according to the working of His great might that He worked in Christ when He raised him from the dead and seated him at His right hand in the heavenly places, far above all rule and authority and power and dominion, and above every name that is named, not only in this age but also in the one to come. And He put all things under his feet and gave him as head over all things to the church, which is his body, the fullness of him who fills all in all—* Ephesians 1:16-23

---

[235] Matthew 28:18

Paul gives the reader a great deal of evidence proving without even the slightest of a doubt that the Father is God alone.

The first statement that reveals this is that all of the requests he presents are directed toward *the Father of glory*, which unquestionably does not in any way speak of someone other than the one he gives this title.

The words directly preceding this statement tells us exactly who *the Father of Glory* is and who he is praying and giving thanks to, *"the God of our lord Jesus Christ"*. The apostle in this prayer mentions these things that are directly associated with the God of Jesus; that He *may give you a spirit of wisdom and of revelation in the knowledge of Him*, we *may know what is the hope to which He has called you, what are the riches of His glorious inheritance in the saints, what is the immeasurable greatness of His power toward us who believe,* and that we know it was by *His great might that He worked in Christ when He raised him from the dead and seated him at His right hand in the heavenly places, far above all rule and authority and power and dominion, and above every name that is named* . Thus, it is clearly understood here that all authority belongs to *the Father of glory* who is *the God of Jesus*. This passage is similar to the accounts contained in first Corinthians chapter fifteen, Philippians chapter two verses nine through eleven, and Colossians chapter one verses nine through eighteen.

Furthermore, it is easily confirmed throughout the New Testament that the Father exalted Jesus and sat him at His right hand as these scriptures tell the reader. In first Peter we also find Jesus being at the right hand of God, *"(he) has gone into heaven and is at the right hand of God, with angels, authorities, and powers having been subjected to him"*[236]. This reinforces the fact that before his ascension into heaven these things were not yet subject to him, which was seen in verses twenty through twenty-three in Ephesians.

It should also be noted that when the apostle speaks of giving thanks to his God, there is no scriptural support that would permit this to refer to anyone other than the Father. This God is our Father, the God of Jesus Christ.

The final thing to point out is this statement that is also said several times throughout the New Testament, *"He raised him from the dead and seated him at His right hand in the heavenly places (then) He put all things under his feet and gave him as head over all things to the church"*. If we assess this with logic, shows that there must be one who has greater authority than Jesus, because the texts says that he was *raised from the dead, seated at His right hand,* and this person *put all things under his feet and gave him head over all things to the church*. With this consider there is no other conclusion that can be

---

[236] 1 Peter 3:22

formed except that this person is *"the God of our Lord Jesus Christ, the Father of glory"*.

15. *The one who conquers and who keeps my works until the end, to him I will give authority over the nations, and he will rule them with a rod of iron, as when earthen pots are broken in pieces, even as I myself have received authority from my Father—Revelation 2:26-27*

These are the words of Jesus himself as he is sitting at the right hand of God. It is important that he here says he received authority from his Father because of all of the references that say his Father is his God as well. Several of these occur in Revelation. This is an instance where the Father gives Jesus the permission to give authority to others, *"Blessed and holy is the one who shares in the first resurrection! Over such the second death has no power, but they will be priests of God and of Christ, and they will reign with him for a thousand years"*. In this verse John informs us we will rule with the messiah for a thousand years, but as was formerly shown, this will be a temporary position until all of the enemies of God are placed under the messiah's feet.

16. *And I heard a loud voice in heaven, saying, "Now the salvation and the power and the kingdom of our God and the authority of His Christ have come, for the accuser of our brothers has been thrown down, who accuses them day and night before our God—Revelation 12:10*

In observing this verse, John tells the reader something noteworthy he heard in heaven, *"the salvation and the power and the kingdom of our God and the authority of His Christ have come"*. This proclamation unmistakably reveals that the Christ is given authority by the God of those who are speaking, which negates the possibility of another being/person to be considered God. To give more clarification to this we find that the verses mentioned previously explain who their God is, the Father. Moreover, this text gives an additional detail. Twice the writer mentions *"our God",* as well as telling us that *the Christ* belongs to the God of those speaking, for it says, *"the authority of His Christ"*. Last of all, John here shows us three things associated with God: God's kingdom, we are accused before God and the Christ is Gods. It should be easily recognized from these illustrations that there is but one person who is God.

8 Through or in Jesus

There can be no debate that God uses what He desires to accomplish His plans, this truth is no different with Jesus. One of the most beloved New Testament verses tells us *"for God so loved the world He gave..."*[237] which I am sure even unbelievers can quote. I'm sure it is engrained in all of our minds that the only way we can have eternal life is through what God gave, Jesus, the son of God. There is nothing more important to know than this fact. But a problem arises when the professed multi-person deity is forced into the word God here, because you cannot pick and choose when it applies to one or the other or all of them. This fictional triune Divine being cannot be a *He*.

In the next verse of chapter three, John says *"God did not send His son...."* which again shows the God he is speaking of must be a *He* that sent. It cannot linguistically be said *God sent His* if indeed Jesus is included in the God that sent, He must then be an *it* or *they* for that to be possible.

The verse seventeen ending explains why the son was sent by God, *"in order that the world might be saved through him"*,[238] showing the messiah was used by Him for a specific purpose.

---
[237] John 3:16

The point in all of this is to show that it is a *Him* that gave *His* son to accomplish *His* will. The conclusion then is that this God must be a *Father* because it is a *son* who is given; thus, God is the Father alone. So, the task at hand in this chapter is to show Jesus is a medium God (the Father) used/uses to do His will, as the example given represents, and he himself is not God.

The first passage I want to address is from Romans chapter three where Paul writes, *"But now the righteousness of God has been manifested apart from the law, although the Law and the Prophets bear witness to it- the righteousness of God through faith in Jesus Christ for all who believe. For there is no distinction: for all have sinned and fall short of the glory of God, and are justified by his grace as a gift, through the redemption that is in Christ Jesus, whom God put forward as a propitiation by his blood, to be received by faith. This was to show God's righteousness, because in his divine forbearance he had passed over former sins".*[239] Every true believer understands that righteousness is not earned, it is a gift. But this is not just righteousness though, it is the righteousness of God. This passage gives the means through which we receive this gift, in/through Jesus Christ. But it must be recognized that it is God's grace through Jesus that He, as the passage says, *"put forward as a*

---

[238] you can also look at John 17:3 to substantiate this
[239] Romans 3:21-25

propitiation by his blood, to be received by faith". It was not the son that gave the gift, but as John wrote in his gospel *""For <u>God so loved the world</u>, that he gave his only Son, that whoever believes in him should not perish but have eternal life. God did not send his Son into the world to condemn the world, but in order that the world might be saved through him"*.[240] The importance in this is that both of these apostles' state God gave the messiah. If God were to be understood as three persons, then *He* cannot be applied to the term because it would make God an *us*. Scripture always says Jesus is God's son without exception, never God or God the son.

1. Therefore, since we have been justified by faith, we have peace with God through our Lord Jesus Christ. Through him we have also obtained access by faith into this grace in which we stand, and we rejoice in hope of the glory of God—Romans 5:1-2

The apostle makes a clear statement that the faith which justifies us gives us peace with God. In speaking of what the object of that faith is in, he says it is *"our lord Jesus Christ"*. Within this verse there are two persons involved, God and Jesus Christ. This is apparent because our peace is *with* God *through our* lord. Verses ten and eleven of this chapter build on this saying, *"or if while we were enemies we were reconciled to God by the death of his Son, much more, now that we are reconciled, shall we be saved*

---

[240] John 3:16-17

by his life. More than that, we also rejoice in God through our Lord Jesus Christ, through whom we have now received reconciliation".[241] It continues speaking of reconciliation we receive through Jesus as the previous passage does. But it also makes it even clearer who Jesus Christ is, God's son. He mentions the resurrection as well saying we are *"saved by his life".*

We know from the rest of scripture that Jesus was raised by God, who the apostle informs us once again, is Jesus's Father.

As Paul finishes verse eleven he tells us of another thing we do through Jesus, we rejoice in God[242] who *"gives us the victory through our Lord Jesus Christ"*[243] because *"There is therefore now no condemnation for those who are in Christ Jesus",*[244] allowing grace to *"reign through righteousness leading to eternal life".*[245]

As I stated previously, it is faith in the messiah that justifies us. But the result of this is peace with God and not the messiah, for it is through the messiah that we receive this peace. That leaves no other alternative but accept the messiah is not God.

---

[241] Romans 5:10-11
[242] Paul says in verse 2 of chapter five that *"we rejoice in hope of the glory of God"*
[243] 1Corinthians 15:57
[244] Romans 8:1
[245] Romans 5:21

12. Now to him who is able to strengthen you according to my gospel and the preaching of Jesus Christ, according to the revelation of the mystery that was kept secret for long ages but has now been disclosed and through the prophetic writings has been made known to all nations, according to the command of the eternal God, to bring about the obedience of faith-to the only wise God be glory forevermore through Jesus Christ! Amen (1Corinthians 16:25-27)

We can see here the very thing Jesus told his disciples, to make known the gospel to all nations, *"Thus it is written, that the Christ should suffer and on the third day rise from the dead, and that repentance and forgiveness of sins should be proclaimed in his name to all nations, beginning from Jerusalem"*.[246] This though is a commandment given to Jesus by the eternal God, as he said *"I do as the Father has commanded me..."*[247] of which he says *"...the word that you hear is not mine but the Father's who sent me"*[248]. In these several verses there is again a *through Jesus* statement.

The first thing though I want to focus on is the mention of *the eternal God*. We are told that He is the one who made known the hidden secret of the gospel that was hidden in the Old Testament. Jesus is the one the Father made this hidden secret known as

---

[246] Luke 24:46
[247] John 14:31
[248] John 14:24

Hebrews chapter one verses one and two say *"Long ago, at many times and in many ways, God spoke to our fathers by the prophets, but in these last days he has spoken to us by his Son, whom he appointed the heir of all things, through whom also he created the world[249]"*. So, this presents Jesus as a means used by the eternal God, not God himself.

To further establish this Paul tells the Corinthians we give glory *to the only wise God* through Jesus for all of the things mentioned in these verses.[250]

I also want to submit that the earlier passages in first Corinthians show irrefutably that Paul is referring to the Father alone as the eternal and only wise God. These passages are: chapter one verse three in which he writes *"Grace to you and peace from God our Father and the Lord Jesus Christ"*, telling us God is our Father, something he greets each assembly with, chapter eight verses four and six when he says *"...an idol has no real existence,"* and that *"there is no God but one...yet for us there is one God, the Father, from whom are all things and for whom we exist..."*, and lastly from chapter fifteen verse twenty four *"Afterwards, the end—whensoever he delivereth up the kingdom unto his God and Father, whensoever he shall bring to nought all rule and all authority and power"*.[251]

---

[249] Hebrews 1:1-2 The word here translated as *world* should be *ages*

[250] this same statement "to the only wise God be glory forevermore through Jesus Christ" is also made in Romans 16:27

[251] Rotherham Emphasized Bible

13. All this is from God, who through Christ reconciled us to Himself and gave us the ministry of reconciliation; that is, in Christ God was reconciling the world to Himself, not counting their trespasses against them, and entrusting to us the message of reconciliation—2Corinthians 5:18-19

In this passage Paul writes *God, who through Christ reconciled us to Himself,* something which he also says in Colossians chapter one verses nineteen and twenty *"For God was pleased to have all His fullness dwell in the Son and through him to reconcile all things to Himself by making peace through the blood of his cross – through him, whether things on earth or things in heaven"*[252]. Yet again we see that the messiah is the agent that God works through. And because God reconciles us through Jesus our trespasses are not held against us. Amen.

As was seen in first Corinthians, it can be firmly established here as well, that the title God is in no way attached to any person other than the Father. The evidence for this begins at the opening of the letter where the apostle writes, *"Blessed be the God and Father of our Lord Jesus Christ, the Father of mercies and God of all comfort"*. As further support he also writes in chapter eleven verse thirty-one, *"The*

---

[252] New English Translation. In their translation notes they say, "The noun "God" does not appear in the Greek text, but since God is the one who reconciles the world to himself (cf. 2 Cor 5:19), he is clearly the subject of εὐδόκησεν (eudokhsen)". The reason I chose to use this translation is because it clarifies who the subject is.

God and Father of the Lord Jesus, He who is blessed forever, knows that I am not lying". The most telling of these[253] is when he states *"the Father of mercies and God of all comfort"* when describing *the God and Father of our Lord Jesus Christ*. This statement cannot be upheld as true if indeed there are multiple persons who are the *"God of all comfort"*, for it clearly says that *the Father of mercies*, a singular person, is the *God of all comfort*.

The conclusion then can only be that *the God and Father of our Lord Jesus Christ, the Father of mercies and God of all comfort* is through Christ *reconciling the world to Himself.*

14. But God, being rich in mercy, because of the great love with which He loved us, even when we were dead in our trespasses, made us alive together with Christ-by grace you have been saved- and raised us up with him and seated us with him in the heavenly places in Christ Jesus, so that in the coming ages He might show the immeasurable riches of His grace in kindness toward us in Christ Jesus. For by grace you have been saved through faith. And this is not your own doing; it is the gift of God, not a result of works, so that no one may boast. For we are His workmanship, created in Christ Jesus for good works, which God prepared beforehand, that we should walk in them—Ephesians 2:4-10

---

[253] This of course is a lesser proof than the obvious *"God and Father of...Jesus"*, of which I find no need to point out

Here we find God and Jesus both have singular personal pronouns attached to them, for God it is *He* and *His*, and for Jesus *him*. This would understandably create two persons, with only one who is said to be God. Moreover, this shows that Jesus is not equal to God as can be seen in this statement *"God...because of the great love with which He loved us...raised us up with him"*, him referring to Jesus. Because this is so, it can be seen that only *God*, the singular person, has these things equated with Him; rich in mercy, great love and grace, made us alive, raised us with Christ, seated us with Christ, gave grace as a gift, we are His workmanship and He prepared good works for us to walk in. In contrast to this, the messiah is said to be; raised up, seated, the source through which we receive grace and kindness, and the means in which we are created for good works. This clearly shows the distinctness between the two persons of God and Jesus.

To makes this more evident, the writer says in verses two and three of chapter one, *"Grace to you and peace from God our Father and the Lord Jesus Christ. Blessed be the God and Father of our Lord Jesus Christ, who has blessed us in Christ with every spiritual blessing in the heavenly places"*. When the author writes *"God our Father"* and *"the God and Father of our lord"*, certainly no prudent person would conclude that the term God in chapter two is different than the person he is speaking of here. One who is judicious can easily recognize what I have offered is true and will find more confidence that it is the Father in the preceding verses that say, *"He chose us in him before the foundation of the world, that we should be holy and blameless before Him. In love He predestined us for adoption as sons through Jesus Christ, according to the purpose of His will, to the praise of His glorious grace, with which He has blessed us in the Beloved"*[254].

The undoubted conclusion from these facts is that what was equated with *God* in chapter two, is logically inclusive of such things seen here that are equated with *God our Father* and *the God and Father of our lord*. Thus, the term *God* is restricted to the Father only.

15. To me, though I am the very least of all the saints, this grace was given, to preach to the Gentiles the unsearchable riches of Christ, and to bring to light for everyone what is the plan of the mystery hidden for ages in God who created all things, so that through the church the manifold wisdom of God might now be made known to the rulers and authorities in the heavenly places. This was according to the eternal purpose that He has realized in Christ Jesus our Lord, in whom we have boldness and access with confidence through our faith in him. So I ask you not to lose heart over what I am suffering for you, which is your glory. For this reason

---

[254] Ephesians 1:4-6

I bow my knees before the Father, from whom every family in heaven and on earth is named, that according to the riches of His glory He may grant you to be strengthened with power through His Spirit in your inner being, so that Christ may dwell in your hearts through faith-that you, being rooted and grounded in love, may have strength to comprehend with all the saints what is the breadth and length and height and depth, and to know the love of Christ that surpasses knowledge, that you may be filled with all the fullness of God—Ephesians 3:8-19

This is the final passage I am going to address in Ephesians pertaining to the subject of this section. I want to start with the verse which says, *"This was according to the eternal purpose that He has realized in Christ Jesus our Lord, in whom we have boldness and access with confidence through our faith in him"*. I am going to look at the context and passages associated with this to conclude what exactly was *realized*, and if we can discover who the *He* in this verse refers to.

Directly associated with the subject of this section we find two mentions of Jesus being the object we receive from God *through*. One, His eternal purpose was realized (accomplished) in him and the second being access to God in him. This eternal purpose Paul speaks about was a hidden mystery, or better said, a secret that was hidden for ages that, as he explains in verse five, *"was not made known to the sons of men in other generations as it has now been revealed to his holy apostles and prophets by the Spirit* and in Romans chapter sixteen, *"Now to him who is able to strengthen you according to my gospel and the preaching of Jesus Christ, according to the revelation of the mystery that was kept secret for long ages but has now been disclosed and through the prophetic writings has been made known to all nations, according to the command of the eternal God, to bring about the obedience of faith- to the only wise God be glory forevermore through Jesus Christ! Amen".*[255] *This secret was hidden for ages in God who created all things.* The secret is the establishment of Jesus' kingdom, the kingdom of God, through his being raised from the dead, which is explained in Colossians chapter one, he is *"the firstborn of all creation. For (in) him all things were created, in heaven and on earth, visible and invisible, whether thrones or dominions or rulers or authorities-all things were created through him and for him. And he is before all things, and in him all things hold together"*[256] and that righteousness is given by faith in this resurrection and his lordship. The reader should also consider Paul says this mystery *was hidden in God who created all things.* This is significant because it was this being's eternal purpose.

As he continues to write, the passage says, *"I bow my knees before the Father, from whom every family*

---

[255] Romans 16:25-27
[256] Colossians 1:15-17

in heaven and on earth is named, that according to the riches of His glory He may grant you to be strengthened with power through His Spirit in your inner being in your inner being..." This specifically shows that when he speaks of God, the Father is who he is directing the reader to. Interesting as well is that he writes, *"strengthened with power through His Spirit"*. From this the supposed personhood of the Spirit must be reject, it is the Fathers spirit. This is verified in Matthews's gospel when Jesus says, *"For it is not you who speak, but the Spirit of your Father speaking through you"*[257].

We find then from the study of the whole of scripture, that the Spirit of God is also called the Fathers Spirit, nullifying the possibility of it being a person/being.

The last thing I want to highlight is the statement *"that you may be filled with all the fullness of God"*.

Often this verse quoted from Colossians chapter one verse nineteen, *"for in him all the fullness of God was pleased to dwell..."* is used as evidence for prove that Jesus is God. But that just isn't so, as can be seen in the proceeding verse, *"and through him to reconcile to Himself all things, whether on earth or in heaven, making peace by the blood of his cross"*.

To put all of this together and explain how erroneous it is to make this claim, I'll start with the statement from Ephesians. Paul desired for the

---

[257] Matthew 10:20

Ephesian believers to be filled with the fullness of God, giving the idea it is achievable. Taking that into consideration, when in in Colossians he *says, "in him all the fullness of God was pleased to dwell"*, this in no way suggests him to be God, otherwise we to can reach that status as well. Furthermore, this is not the only way this is translated as this list of several know translations show:

- *For it pleased the Father that in him should all fullness dwell—King James*
- *For it was the good pleasure of the Father that in him should all the fullness dwell—American Standard Version*
- *For God was pleased to have all his fullness dwell in the Son—NET*
- *Because in him it did please all the fullness to tabernacle—Young's Literal Translation*

The idea of *Father* or *God*, though not contained in the Greek text[258], is correct, seeing He is the one who does the reconciliation as second Corinthians chapter five verse eighteen shows, *"all this is from God, who through Christ reconciled us to himself"*.

So again, as second Corinthians substantiates, Jesus is the one through which God accomplishes his purposes and plans.

16. And the peace of God, which surpasses all understanding, will guard your hearts and your minds in Christ Jesus—Philippians 4:7

---

[258] The literal rendering is seen in Young's translation

Peace of God is something Paul alludes to often in his letters such as Romans chapter fifteen verse thirty-three *"May the God of peace be with you all"*, showing we receive the peace of God from the God of peace. In his greetings *God our Father* us used, not *God the Father* as many would suggest it to be understood, to teach us that God is our Father[259].

In addition to this, as is the purpose of this section, he once again shows that it is *in/through* Jesus that we receive something from God. In this instance it is *the peace of God*, which we find in Romans chapter five comes through his mediation for us, *"Therefore, since we have been justified by faith, we have peace with God through our Lord Jesus Christ"*.[260]

17. If then you have been raised with Christ, seek the things that are above, where Christ is, seated at the right hand of God—Colossians 3:1

Yet again the apostle is found telling the reader that Christ has risen, and he is *seated at the right hand of God*, which, by the way, is quite important in recognizing who God consists of.

Why was he seated at the right hand of God, because he is God? That isn't what scripture tells us. Rather, we see as one example in Acts chapter two verse thirty-six Peter says, *"God has made him both Lord and Christ, this Jesus whom you crucified"*.[261]

---

[259] This phrase is usually followed by *"and our lord Jesus Christ"*
[260] Romans 5:1

Peter also speaks about this in chapter five of Acts, *"The God of our fathers raised Jesus, whom you killed by hanging him on a tree. God exalted him at his right hand as Leader and Savior, to give repentance to Israel and forgiveness of sins"*.[262]

So, it is clear that Jesus was exalted, or lifted up to the glory he was predestined to have as foretold by David, who *"being a prophet, and knowing that God had sworn with an oath to him that he would set one of his descendants on his throne, he foresaw and spoke about the resurrection of the Christ, that he was not abandoned to Hades, nor did his flesh see corruption"*.[263]

But the main point the apostle is making is we to have been raised with Jesus, though not yet in a physical way. This without doubt refers to baptism and what it represents, a sign of death and renewal of life as he explains in verse three, *"For you have died, and your life is hidden with Christ in God"*. This also speaks of the messiah's mediatorial position as he writes in Romans, *"Christ Jesus is the one who died- more than that, who was raised-who is at the right hand of God, who indeed is interceding for us"*.[264]

So, only because Jesus was raised from the dead and exalted by God can we be raised to the newness

---

[261] Considering Jesus was *made lord and Christ*, this would necessitate that he did not have those titles prior to his resurrection
[262] Acts 5:30-31
[263] Acts 2:31-32
[264] Romans 8:34

of life as well as the future resurrection. He is the means by which these things are given to us by God.

18. Let the word of Christ dwell in you richly, teaching and admonishing one another in all wisdom, singing psalms and hymns and spiritual songs, with thankfulness in your hearts to God. And whatever you do, in word or deed, do everything in the name of the Lord Jesus, giving thanks to God the Father through him—Colossians 3:16-17

I find this pretty interesting because Paul says, *"to give thanks to God the Father through him"*. The reason being, we are never told to give thanks to anyone other than the Father, this being one of the many proofs. Furthermore, we are told to *do everything in the name of...Jesus*, and then are given instructions to give thanks to God through him. Jesus is not the God we give thanks to, His Father is.[265]

When looking at these verses the first thing I want to bring to the surface is a discrepancy in the different Greek texts from verse sixteen. The Textus Receptus reads καρδίαις υμων τω κυριω *(your heart to the Lord)*, whereas Tischendorf and Wescott Hort read καρδίαις υμων τω θεω *(your heart to God)*, which does give the possibility of a difference in who the singing is addressed to, either God or the messiah. It should though, be obvious that it is referring to

---

[265] We find Jesus himself giving thanks to the Father, with Matthew 11:25 and Luke 10:21 being the most definitive concerning his view of the Father.

God due to the ending of verse seventeen, *"giving thanks to God the Father through him"*.

The ending of verse seventeen is translated several different ways because the definite article *the* is not attached to Father, along with the absence of *kai* (and) connecting the two words. Here are how they read: Rotherhams Emphasized Version, *the Divine Father*, the King James, *God and the Father,* and Young's Literal Translation, *the God and Father.*

Literally it says *"to the God Father"* which in my opinion Rotherham's translation catches the idea being portrayed. Our God is our divine Father. With this in mind, it should be (sadly not *is*) easily established, whichever way it is translated, that Jesus is why we live, speak and praise our God and Father who sent him.

19. For God has not destined us for wrath, but to obtain salvation through our Lord Jesus Christ, who died for us so that whether we are awake or asleep we might live with him—1Thessalonians 5:9-10

Contained within these two verses are several things that make a clear distinction between the word *God* and any other person mentioned in the passage, namely Jesus. The apostle tells the reader that *"God has not destined us for wrath, but to obtain salvation"*, showing the opposing results for belief and unbelief. We are also told that this salvation is gained *"through our Lord Jesus Christ"*.

In examining these two statements, a determination that Jesus is not included in the person of God can noticeably be seen. The writer tells us God has not destined to one thing but the other, whereas it is *through our Lord Jesus Christ* that God destined us to be saved. Thus, we have God being one person and our Lord being the other. By attaching *our* to *Lord Jesus Christ*, he must be eliminated from the possibility of being an additional person within the being of God, because *God* saves through *our*.

To further support this, Paul writes in chapter one *"remembering before our God and Father your work of faith and labor of love and steadfastness of hope in our Lord Jesus Christ"*[266], showing that God is *our Father*.

The last thing I want to mention comes from the statement *"Jesus...died for us"*. Because God is the one who destined us to be saved, the only logical conclusion can be that He is not the one who died to obtain what was destined for us to receive.

Furthermore, God, or more specifically, the God of our Lord,[267] is the one who raised him that died for us from the dead. Judging the evidence presented the reader can see that the apostle reminds us that our God and Father destined us for salvation through our messiah's death and resurrection.

---

[266] 1Thessalonians 1:3
[267] Ephesians 1:16-21

20. But we ought always to give thanks to God for you, brothers beloved by the Lord, because God chose you as the firstfruits to be saved, through sanctification by the Spirit and belief in the truth. To this He called you through our gospel, so that you may obtain the glory of our Lord Jesus Christ—2Thessalonians 2:13-14

The apostle does not here specifically say the Father when he uses the word God, but the word is set apart from the other two supposed persons of the multi-person God. In this passage the spirit and Jesus are portrayed as objects God uses to work through and bring about His will; by the spirit he desires to sanctify us and through Jesus we are called to obtain the glory he was given.[268] As evidence for this, the apostle says, *"we ought always to give thanks to God"*, a statement he says often in his letters. One of the numerous examples is found in first Thessalonians chapter one verses two and three where he says *"We give thanks to God always for all of you, constantly mentioning you in our prayers, remembering before our God and Father your work of faith and labor of love and steadfastness of hope in our Lord Jesus Christ"*. You can also see this in chapter two verse twelve of first Thessalonians, *"so that the name of our Lord Jesus may be glorified in you, and you in him, according to the grace of our God and the Lord Jesus Christ"*. The two are definitely described as different persons when he

---

[268] the glory of Jesus

writes *our God* and *Jesus* as singular individuals. I applied these specific verses to this passage because they are written to the same assembly, which helps to determine how Paul understood the personhood of God.

This passages also contains the use of *our* when referring to the messiah, as in *our Lord*. This has already been spoken of in an earlier exposition, so I would refer the reader to the verses directly above.

Pertaining to *the Spirit,* I have addressed that as well in Ephesians chapter three verses eight through nineteen. So yet again it is established that the only one who is God is our Father.

21. But when the goodness and loving kindness of God our Savior appeared, He saved us, not because of works done by us in righteousness, but according to His own mercy, by the washing of regeneration and renewal of the Holy Spirit, whom He poured out on us richly through Jesus Christ our Savior, so that being justified by His grace we might become heirs accord-ing to the hope of eternal life—Titus 3:4-7

There seems to be somewhat of a predicament here if indeed we are to understand that *savior* can only be applied to God. The problem with this theory is it is totally unbiblical. The very name of Jesus[269] means YHWH's salvation. Salvation is always credited to God, yet there are many who are called

---

[269] Most scholars agree that the name he was given by YHWH is Yeshua, which is said to be a shortened form of Yehoshua

saviors seen in the book of Judges. Moreover, scripture tells us that God raised these people up to be saviors, which is exactly why Jesus is given the title savior. This is revealed when the angel tells Mary *"for he will save his people from their sins"*.[270]

Thus, it is through Jesus we receive salvation, and this because of his obedience which in turn gave him the glory to be the first eternally raised from the dead. He is savior because of his obedience to the one who sent him to save us. God is given all credit and glory by Paul, it is His loving kindness, He saved us, it is His mercy, He poured out the spirit and we are justified by His grace. So ultimately God is the savior and Jesus is His tool used to save.

We do find in scripture that Jesus is said to pour out the spirit, but it is only because He *"received from the Father the promise of the Holy Spirit, (that) he has poured out this that you yourselves are seeing and hearing"*[271]. So, we find then the same theme, it is actually God who pours out the Spirit, but He does so by Jesus.

Another important thing to note pertaining to Paul saying *God our savior* and *Jesus Christ our savior.* that is *God our savior…poured out…through Jesus Christ our savior,* show that the one who poured out is not the one who this was done through. Thus, God, the singular person[272] who is described as

---

[270] Matthew 1:21
[271] Acts 2:36
[272] This is attested to by the use of He and His

our Father in chapter one, is separated from all other persons.

22. Now may the God of peace who brought again from the dead our Lord Jesus, the great shepherd of the sheep, by the blood of the eternal covenant, equip you with everything good that you may do His will, working in us that which is pleasing in His sight, through Jesus Christ, to whom be glory forever and ever. Amen.—Hebrew 13:20-21

The writer of Hebrews starts of saying here *"the God of peace who brought again from the dead our lord Jesus"*. This produces a strong objection to the idea of Jesus himself being God.

In first Thessalonians chapter five verse twenty-three the apostle Paul says this *"Now may the God of peace Himself sanctify you completely, and may your whole spirit and soul and body be kept blameless at the coming of our Lord Jesus Christ"*. These verses show the God of peace is not our lord Jesus, nor can he be included in God, seeing that God brought him from the dead. The writer of Hebrews appears to understand that Jesus is the mediator, the go between that is ever present before God on our behalf because it is through him we are equipped *"with everything good that you may do His will, working in us that which is pleasing in His sight"*. Lastly, it is to *the God of peace…who brought our Lord* from the dead that the apostle says *be glory forever and ever.*

In the first letter of Peter there are several mentions of God working through Jesus that I want to address. In the first he writes *"you...like living stones are being built up as a spiritual house, to be a holy priesthood, to offer spiritual sacrifices acceptable to God through Jesus Christ"*.[273] This is not a new idea, that is, God's people being His priesthood. In Exodus chapter nineteen YHWH said to Israel after leaving Egypt that, *"If you will indeed obey my voice and keep my covenant, you shall be my treasured possession among all peoples, for all the earth is mine; and you shall be to me a kingdom of priests and a holy nation"*[274] which did not pan out though because of their disobedience. Yet this was still what He desired for those that would trust in Him as Isaiah proclaims *"And some of them also I will take for priests and for Levites, says the Lord. "For as the new heavens and the new earth that I make shall remain before me, says the Lord, so shall your offspring and your name remain"*.[275] In Revelation John writes in chapter one verse six that through Jesus we are made *"a kingdom, priests to his God and Father, to him be glory and dominion forever and ever. Amen"*, with a major emphasis I might add on *"to his God and Father"*. In chapter five verse ten there is also the four living creatures and twenty-four elders saying, *"you have made them a kingdom and priests to our God, and they shall reign on the*

---

[273] 1 Peter 2:5
[274] Exodus 19:5-6
[275] Isaiah 66:21-22

earth." An important thing to notice is that Jesus made us priests, but the question is how, because he is God? Well verse five of Revelation gives the answer, *"and from Jesus Christ the faithful witness, the firstborn of the dead, and the ruler of kings on earth. To him who loves us and has freed us from our sins by his blood"*. It is only because of his obedient death and resurrection. According to Peter we are to *offer up spiritual sacrifices acceptable to God,* which is done through Jesus. So, we are made a kingdom of priests because of Jesus, and we offer these sacrifices through him unto God.

As I mentioned, an emphasis must be put on the statement *"unto his God and Father"* because this is the one he made us a kingdom of priests to. Taking that into account I would think it to be obvious that YHWH is his God and Father. Once again, the common thread throughout the apostolic writings is that it is *through* Jesus or *in* Jesus, we can approach God.

Later in Peters first epistle in chapter four verses ten through eleven he tells the readers that God is also glorified through Jesus saying, *"as each has received a gift, use it to serve one another, as good stewards of God's varied grace: whoever speaks, as one who speaks oracles of God; whoever serves, as one who serves by the strength that God supplies-in order that in everything God may be glorified through Jesus Christ. To him belong glory and dominion forever and ever. Amen"*. The apostle here also tells us that to this God belongs *dominion forever and ever* which he also states in chapter five verses ten through eleven which reads *"after you have suffered a little while, the God of all grace, who has called you to his eternal glory in Christ, will himself restore, confirm, strengthen, and establish you. To him be the dominion forever and ever. Amen."* In his words from chapter five, *"the God of all grace has called you to His eternal glory in Christ"*, there should be no confusion as to who he does not describe as God, Christ. But when going back to verse three of chapter one it can be substantiated that the use of God and who it refers to according to Peter is *the God and Father of our Lord Jesus Christ.* This is even further confirmed by Peters preaching in Acts, in which he always proclaiming God to be greater than Jesus as well as the one whom He worked/works through such as *"Jesus of Nazareth, a man attested to you by God with mighty works and wonders and signs that God did through him in your midst, as you yourselves know"* in chapter two verse twenty-two. This is one of Jesus's closets disciples, so I find it very perplexing that he would say such things if indeed the messiah is God. Obviously, Peter rejects that nonsensical philosophical bologna.

23. And we know that the Son of God has come and has given us understanding, so that we may know Him who is true; and we are in Him who is true, in

His Son Jesus Christ. He is the true God and eternal life—1 John 5:20

I believe much of what John writes is misunderstood by most who read the scriptures. This is a case that shows why I feel this way.

First though I want to focus on what this section is about. John writes that *"we are in Him who is true"*, which is reminiscent of what he says in his gospel *"that they may all be one, just as you, Father, are in me, and I in you, that they also may be in us, so that the world may believe that you have sent me"*[276]. This shows the fulfillment of what Jesus requested from his Father, that we be in them both.

When speaking of being in Him who is true and His son, Jesus gives an explanation of what he means by this in John's gospel, *"If you abide in my word, you are truly my disciples, and you will know the truth, and the truth will set you free."*[277] When he tells them to abide in my word, this word is actually his Fathers as he says *"Whoever does not love me does not keep my words. And the word that you hear is not mine but the Father's who sent me"*[278] and *"I have given them your word…"*[279]. We also see that the truth that sets us free is found when Jesus also says, *"Sanctify them in the truth; your word is truth"*[280].

---

[276] John 17:21
[277] John 8:31-32
[278] John 14:24
[279] John 17:14
[280] John 17:17

So, we find then that our understanding of God is given through the word He gave through His son.

Additionally, I notice a statement that is very similar to something John says in chapter seventeen of his gospel, *this is eternal life, that they know you, the only true God...* The similarity if found where he writes *He is the true God and eternal life*. These both are speaking of the same person, the Father. This is seen in his gospel because Jesus specifically says *Father*, and here by the phrase *His son*.

To further establish this, here are some telling things John says of *He who is the true God*: *the Son of God has come and has given us understanding, so that we may know Him who is true* and *we are in Him who is true, in His Son Jesus Christ*. This tells the reader that *the true God* is *Him who is true* and that *we are in Him who is true*. So, seeing that in His (*Him who is true*) son we are in *Him who is true*, we can logically conclude *the son* is not *Him who is true*, thus, *the true God and eternal life* is the Father. Any other determination is fully ridiculous and unfounded.

9 Jesus is a Man

The fact that Jesus was a man is not a disputed issue, the problem that arises comes from the claim he is the God-man, one hundred percent God and one hundred percent man.[281] But is that what scripture teaches?

There is nowhere in scripture where anyone claims him to be both God and man, unless of course verses are broken away from the context to do so. Scripture always speaks of Jesus as the *son of God* or *the son of man* or the prophet Moses spoke of, all prophetic references to the messiah. The Pharisees and all of the other Hebrews of the first century understood these titles, as can be seen in statements and questions such as *"I adjure you by the living God, tells if you are the Christ, the Son of God"*[282] and *"This is indeed the Prophet who is to come into the world!" Perceiving then that they were about to come and take him by force to make him king, Jesus withdrew again to the mountain by himself".*[283]

Before I get to the passages that clearly call Jesus a man, I want to point out references alluding to

---

[281] I find it amazing that the laws of mathematics can be cast aside to justify a doctrine. You cannot be 100% of this and 100% of something completely opposite
[282] Matthew 26:63
[283] John 6:14

people seeing Jesus as a man alone. I'll begin with Matthew chapter eight when Jesus heals the Centurions servant who says to Jesus, *"For I too am a man under authority, with soldiers under me. And I say to one, 'Go,' and he goes, and to another, 'Come,' and he comes, and to my servant, 'Do this,' and he does it"*.[284] The implication comes from the centurions saying *I too am a man.* He understood that Jesus was a man with great authority, and it appears that he believed he was a king (maybe even the messianic king).

Nicodemus also recognized where this authority came from saying, *"Rabbi, we know that you are a teacher come from God, for no one can do these signs that you do unless God is with him"*[285], as does Peter in Acts chapter ten, *"how God anointed Jesus of Nazareth with the Holy Spirit and with power. He went about doing good and healing all who were oppressed by the devil, for God was with him"*.[286] Jesus himself tells his disciples this very thing after his resurrection, saying *"All authority in heaven and on earth has been given to me"*.[287] Notice he says *has been given to me*, making it clear he had never possessed this authority, otherwise he would say *has been given back to me.*

---

[284] Matthew 8:9
[285] John 3:2
[286] Acts 10:38
[287] Matthew 28:18

Another example is a dialogue between Jesus and a Samaritan woman in Johns gospel, *"Sir, I perceive that you are a prophet. Our fathers worshiped on this mountain, but you say that in Jerusalem is the place where people ought to worship." Jesus said to her, "Woman, believe me, the hour is coming when neither on this mountain nor in Jerusalem will you worship the Father. You worship what you do not know; we worship what we know, for salvation is from the Jews. But the hour is coming, and is now here, when the true worshipers will worship the Father in spirit and truth, for the Father is seeking such people to worship him. God is spirit, and those who worship him must worship in spirit and truth."*.[288] This in and of itself shows Jesus himself say he worships the Father[289] as do the other religious Jews, explaining clearly who God is. There is no doubt in a logical and sane mind that God does not worship Himself, but rather is worshipped by what He created. So, Jesus is unquestionably a man and not God.

In John chapter nine verses thirty-one through thirty-three a man whose sight was restored said this to the Pharisees, *"We know that God does not listen to sinners, but if anyone is a worshiper of God and does his will, God listens to him. Never since the world began has it been heard that anyone opened*

---

[288] John 4:19-24

[289] As can be heard in his statement *"true worshipers will worship the Father in spirit and truth... God is spirit, and those who worship him must worship in spirit and truth"*

the eyes of a man born blind. If this man were not from God, he could do nothing". Here once again, Jesus is said to worship God, along with doing His will, which is why God listened to him[290]. When we come to the ending of this passage, the once blind man says Jesus is from God. This is exactly what Jesus confessed multiple times, such as this account the writer of the gospel relates, *"Jesus, knowing that the Father had given all things into his hands, and that he had come from God and was going back to God"*.[291]

John's gospel has many other references showing Jesus to be a man[292], here is a list of some,

- *"So the woman left her water jar and went away into town and said to the people, "Come, see a man who told me all that I ever did. Can this be the Christ?"(4:28-29)*,
- *"So the Jews said to the man who had been healed, "It is the Sabbath, and it is not lawful for you to take up your bed." But he answered them, "The man who healed me, that man said to me, 'Take up your bed, and walk.'" They asked him, "Who is the man who said to you, 'Take up your bed and walk'?"(5:10-12)*

---

[290] This can be seen in John 11:41-42 *"Father, I thank you that you have heard me. I knew that you always hear me, but I said this on account of the people standing around, that they may believe that you sent me."*

[291] John 13:3

[292] The gospel of John is the main source for those who purport a multi-person God get their text from

- *"The Jews then disputed among themselves, saying, "How can this man give us his flesh to eat?" (6:52)*
- *"And there was much muttering about him among the people. While some said, "He is a good man," others said, "No, he is leading the people astray."(7:12)*
- *"The Jews therefore marveled, saying, "How is it that this man has learning, when he has never studied?"(7:15)*
- *"Some of the people of Jerusalem therefore said, "Is not this the man whom they seek to kill? And here he is, speaking openly, and they say nothing to him! Can it be that the authorities really know that this is the Christ? But we know where this man comes from, and when the Christ appears, no one will know where he comes from."(7:25-27)*
- *"Yet many of the people believed in him. They said, "When the Christ appears, will he do more signs than this man has done?"(7:31)*
- *"The Jews said to one another, "Where does this man intend to go that we will not find him? Does he intend to go to the Dispersion among the Greeks and teach the Greeks?" (7:35)*
- *"The officers answered, "No one ever spoke like this man!" (7:36)*
- *"Does our law judge a man without first giving him a hearing and learning what he does?"*, *"He answered, "The man called Jesus made mud and anointed my eyes and said to me, 'Go to Siloam and*

wash.' So I went and washed and received my sight." (9:11)
- "Some of the Pharisees said, "This man is not from God, for he does not keep the Sabbath." But others said, "How can a man who is a sinner do such signs?" And there was a division among them." (9:16)
- "So, for the second time they called the man who had been blind and said to him, "Give glory to God. We know that this man is a sinner." (9:24)
- "We know that God has spoken to Moses, but as for this man, we do not know where he comes from." (9:29)
- "The Jews answered him, "It is not for a good work that we are going to stone you but for blasphemy, because you, being a man, make yourself God." (10:33)
- "And many came to him. And they said, "John did no sign, but everything that John said about this man was true." (10:41)
- "So the chief priests and the Pharisees gathered the Council and said, "What are we to do? For this man performs many signs. If we let him go on like this, everyone will believe in him, and the Romans will come and take away both our place and our nation." But one of them, Caiaphas, who was high priest that year, said to them, "You know nothing at all. Nor do you understand that it is better for you that one man should die for the people, not that the whole nation should perish." (11:47-50) "It was Caiaphas who had advised the Jews that it would

be expedient that one man should die for the people." (18:14)
- *"The servant girl at the door said to Peter, "You also are not one of this man's disciples, are you?" He said, "I am not." (18:17)*
- *"So Pilate went outside to them and said, "What accusation do you bring against this man? They answered him, "If this man were not doing evil, we would not have delivered him over to you." (18:29-30)*
- *"They cried out again, "Not this man, but Barabbas!" Now Barabbas was a robber." (18:40)*
- *"So Jesus came out, wearing the crown of thorns and the purple robe. Pilate said to them, "Behold the man!" (19:5)*
- *"From then on Pilate sought to release him, but the Jews cried out, "If you release this man, you are not Caesar's friend. Everyone who makes himself a king opposes Caesar." (19:5).*

There are also other scriptures that concur with this. One example is in John chapter eight verse forty when Jesus says *"You seek to kill me, a man who has told you the truth that I heard from God. This is not what Abraham did"*. There is no implication here. He without question says he is a man, and not just a man, but a man who heard the truth from God!

The question has to be asked then. Did he even know what he was if Orthodoxy is true? A man, God, God-man or just plain confused because everyone keeps telling him he's God, some he's a man, and supposedly, he claims to be God one second and the next he is a man.

Jesus says he is *the son of man* seventy-eight times, the *son of man* being a prophetic title for the messiah from Daniel chapter seven verses thirteen and fourteen, *"I saw in the night visions, and behold, with the clouds of heaven there came one like a son of man, and he came to the Ancient of Days and was presented before him. And to him was given dominion and glory and a kingdom, that all peoples, nations, and languages should serve him; his dominion is an everlasting dominion, which shall not pass away, and his kingdom one that shall not be destroyed".*

In Joseph Bensons Commentary of the Old and New Testament he quotes from *Defense of Christianity from the ancient Prophecies,* p. 131 that "*anani,* the clouds, was a known name of the Messiah among the Jewish writers, which shows that they understood this text as spoken of him. Benson also says of this "He particularly alludes to this text, Mat 26:64, where he speaks of his *coming in the clouds of heaven;* by which expression he acknowledged himself to be the true Messiah here described and gave a direct answer to the question there proposed to him, *Art thou the Christ, the Son of the blessed?*".

He is also called the son of God twenty-six times in the gospels, another messianic title from first Chronicles chapter twenty-two verse ten, *"He shall build a house for my name. He shall be my son, and I will be his father, and I will establish his royal throne in Israel forever"*.

All of these titles are interchangeable, yet they refer to the same person, the coming redeemer of Israel.

Further on in the letters of the apostles, the same indication is found. Starting with Romans chapter fifteen verses fifteen, seventeen and nineteen the apostle writes, *"But the free gift is not like the trespass. For if many died through one man's trespass, much more have the grace of God and the free gift by the grace of that one man Jesus Christ abounded for many...For if, because of one man's trespass, death reigned through that one man, much more will those who receive the abundance of grace and the free gift of righteousness reign in life through the one man Jesus Christ... For as by the one man's disobedience the many were made sinners, so by the one man's obedience the many will be made righteous"*. Clearly, Jesus had to be a man, the second Adam.

Paul, in 1Corinthians, gives more insight concerning these verse as to why the messiah had to be a man and not a God-man, where he tells us *"for as by a man came death, by a man has come also the resurrection of the dead. For as in Adam all die, so also in Christ shall all be made alive. But each in his own order: Christ the first fruits, then at his coming those who belong to Christ"*[293] and *"so is it with the resurrection of the dead. What is sown is perishable; what is raised is imperishable. It is sown in dishonor; it is raised in glory. It is sown in weakness; it is raised in power. It is sown a natural body; it is raised a spiritual body. If there is a natural body, there is also a spiritual body. Thus it is written, "The first man Adam became a living being"; the last Adam became a life-giving spirit. But it is not the spiritual that is first but the natural, and then the spiritual. The first man was from the earth, a man of dust; the second man is from heaven. As was the man of dust, so also are those who are of the dust, and as is the man of heaven, so also are those who are of heaven. Just as we have borne the image of the man of dust, we shall also bear the image of the man of heaven".*[294]

To make it even more evident, we know he was tempted as the synoptic gospels show, something that God cannot experience as James makes plain, *"Let no one say when he is tempted, "I am being tempted by God," for God cannot be tempted with evil, and he himself tempts no one."* Being God cannot be tempted, the writer of Hebrews makes it clear he was just as the gospels testify, saying" *therefore he had to be made like his brothers in every respect, so that he might become a merciful and faithful high priest in the service of God, to make propitiation for the sins of the people. For because he himself has suffered when tempted, he is able to help those who are being*

---

[293] 1 Corinthians 15:21-23
[294] 1 Corinthians 15:42-49

tempted" and *"For we do not have a high priest who is unable to sympathize with our weaknesses, but one who in every respect has been tempted as we are, yet without sin."*.[295]

Taking this into account first Corinthians chapter ten verse thirteen would have to be applied to Jesus when Paul says, *"no temptation has overtaken you that is not common to man. God is faithful, and he will not let you be tempted beyond your ability, but with the temptation he will also provide the way of escape, that you may be able to endure it"*. This can be no more expressed than when Jesus in his greatest temptation, knowing what he was to suffer, says to his disciples, *"My soul is very sorrowful, even to death; remain here, and watch with me."* And going a little farther he fell on his face and prayed, saying, *"My Father, if it be possible, let this cup pass from me; nevertheless, not as I will, but as you will."*

It is clear he sought to obey His Fathers will, not his. Thus, you can come away with no other conclusion than Jesus' Father is God alone, for the messiah was and is a man. I want to leave this section with the words of Paul, *"for there is one God, and there is one mediator between God and men, <u>the man Christ Jesus</u>"*.[296]

---

[295] Hebrews 4:15
[296] 1Timothy 2:5

10 Jesus Belongs to God

The idea of Jesus belonging to God seems to be an aspect of the relationship he has with God that is never really mentioned. Considering the idea that God is three persons but one God, I suppose this could be possible seeing it is alleged He is not a singular personal being but rather comprised of three separate personal beings, making God an *it*. For this to be, God being multi-personal, scripture cannot disagree with this theory, and yes that is exactly what it is, a theory.

There are two main verses I want to bring to attention that cause a major problem with this erroneous and dangerous assessment. The first of these is from first Corinthians chapter three verses twenty-one through twenty-three where Paul says, *"so let no one boast in men. For all things are yours, whether Paul or Apollos or Cephas or the world or life or death or the present or the future-all are yours, and you are Christ's, and Christ is God's".*

In the context of this verse Paul numerous times makes mention of God, such as, *"...God gave the growth"* (verse 6), *"...only God who gives the growth"* (verse 7), and *"If anyone destroys God's temple, God will destroy him"* (verse 17). It can be gathered from this that Paul sees God as a distinct being who is the source of these things he mentions. With this in mind, when looking at the ending of verse twenty there is a progression beginning with the Apostles being listed as belonging to and for the benefit of the readers, with the readers and themselves belonging to Christ and Christ belonging to God. Because of the fact that Paul shows a hierarchy, it cannot be much clearer that each one referred to is distinct from the other and leads to the simple conclusion that Christ belonging to God negates the possibility of him being God himself. The one who can be defined as God is the Father of Jesus who Paul says in chapter one verse three is *God our Father*.

Further on in the letter Paul also says in chapter eleven verse three, "*but I want you to understand that the head of every man is Christ, the head of a wife is her husband, and the head of Christ is God*". Paul this time defines the positions of authority possessed by the persons mentioned, with the ultimate head over everyone being God. It seems quite irrational that a person would insist that someone who has a head is equal to his head, and if truth be told, this would have them saying he is his head.

Further in this letter the apostle undoubtedly shows that the singular, not multi person of God, has authority over Jesus, saying in chapter fifteen "*whensoever he delivereth up the kingdom unto his God and Father*"[297] and "*When all things are subjected to him, then the Son himself will also be subjected to him who put all things in subjection under him, that God may be all in all".*

There can be no other logical interpretation than the Father is God alone and Jesus is his son and servant as Hebrews chapter ten verse seven suggests, *"Then I said, 'Behold, I have come to do your will, O God, as it is written of me in the scroll of the book".*

---

[297] Rotherhams Emphasized Bible

11 Jesus is With God, Not is God

Dare I say that there is no person who has read the Bible that would say Jesus is not now with God? I confidently believe not. But the question is how he is with God? Is he now returned to his state of being with God and also being God as many interpret John's gospel to suggest? If so, how is he still a man which informs Mary and his disciples after his resurrection that he is going to his and their God? I find it very difficult to suggest that Jesus, though supposedly God who returned to his glory, still has a God over him as he sits in his eternally possessed position. The fact that he now sits in an authoritative position with God is said numerous times. Yet is that to be taken that he is God? The most common statement about this is the statement *"at the right hand of God"*, thus, suggesting that he is not God as he sits. Here is a list of some of the passages that say this:

- *So then the Lord Jesus, after he had spoken to them, was taken up into heaven and sat down at the right hand of God—Mark 16:19*
- *Being therefore exalted at the right hand of God, and having received from the Father the promise of the Holy Spirit, he has poured out this that you yourselves are seeing and hearing—Acts 2:33*

- *But he, full of the Holy Spirit, gazed into heaven and saw the glory of God, and Jesus standing at the right hand of God—Acts 7:55*
- *Who is to condemn? Christ Jesus is the one who died-more than that, who was raised-who is at the right hand of God, who indeed is interceding for us—Romans 8:34*
- *that he worked in Christ when he raised him from the dead and seated him at his right hand in the heavenly places—Ephesians 1:20*
- *if then you have been raised with Christ, seek the things that are above, where Christ is, seated at the right hand of God—Colossians 3:1*
- *Now the point in what we are saying is this: we have such a high priest, one who is seated at the right hand of the throne of the Majesty in heaven, a minister in the holy places, in the true tent that the Lord set up, not man—Hebrews 8:1-2*
- *But when Christ had offered for all time a single sacrifice for sins, he sat down at the right hand of God, waiting from that time until his enemies should be made a footstool for his feet—Hebrews 10:12-13*
- *looking to Jesus, the founder and perfecter of our faith, who for the joy that was set before him endured the cross, despising the shame, and is seated at the right hand of the throne of God—Hebrews 12:2*

The fact that he sits at the right hand of God is not his doing, it is Gods, as Ephesians chapter one verses seventeen, nineteen and twenty reveal *"the*

God of our Lord Jesus Christ, the Father of glory...according to the working of his great might that he worked in Christ when he raised him from the dead and seated him at his right hand in the heavenly places" This is not the only place that affirms he was exalted by another party, that being God. Other examples are Acts 2:33, 5:31 and Philippians 2:9.

First and second Timothy strongly affirm the fact that Jesus is with God[298] in a very straight forward and undisputable way. In chapter five verse twenty one of first Timothy Paul writes, *"In the presence of God and of Christ Jesus and of the elect angels I charge you to keep these rules without prejudging, doing nothing from partiality"*, in chapter six verses thirteen through sixteen he writes, *"I charge you in the presence of God, who gives life to all things, and of Christ Jesus, who in his testimony before Pontius Pilate made the good confession, to keep the commandment unstained and free from reproach until the appearing of our Lord Jesus Christ, which he will display at the proper time-he who is the blessed and only Sovereign, the King of kings and Lord of lords, who alone has immortality, who dwells in unapproachable light, whom no one has ever seen or can see. To him be honor and eternal dominion. Amen"* and in second Timothy chapter four verses one and two, *"I charge you in the presence of God and of Christ Jesus, who is to judge the living and the*

---

[298] Being that Jesus is with "God" there can be no other conclusion than to say he is not God

dead, and by his appearing and his kingdom: preach the word; be ready in season and out of season; reprove, rebuke, and exhort, with complete patience and teaching". Each one of these have a common thread, Timothy is charged as if he were *in the presence of God and of Christ Jesus* with chapter five adding *the elect angels*. I want to be extremely frank with the reader, what is written here makes the contention that Jesus is God to be complete and utter folly. There are two persons who are said to be considered spiritually present with Timothy and the apostle, that being God and Christ Jesus. It is difficult to accept the likelihood that any person with a reasonable and spiritual mind would deny what is, not implied, but is an in-your-face fact that Jesus is <u>with</u> God. If they were not separate beings/persons, this would be an incredibly baffling statement.

There is also another detail to be brought out. Jesus is to judge the living and the dead. But it can be seen he was appointed judge when looking at Acts chapter seventeen verses thirty and thirty one: *The times of ignorance God overlooked, but now he commands all people everywhere to repent, because he has fixed a day on which he will judge the world in righteousness by a man whom he has appointed; and of this he has given assurance to all by raising him from the dead"*. This makes it crystal clear, <u>God</u> appointed Jesus to judge the living and the dead. This authority was given to him. And not only that, but he is a man whom God raised from the dead.

Furthermore, within the passages there are descriptions of God that are not given to Jesus such as *"who gives life to all things"* and *"he who is the blessed and only Sovereign, the King of kings and Lord of lords, who alone has immortality, who dwells in unapproachable light, whom no one has ever seen or can see. To him be honor and eternal dominion"*. Again, these statements are applied only to God and not Jesus, of which both are present at the same time.

The fact that the Messiah is <u>with</u> God, is seen throughout the New and Old Testament alike. An example is seen in Peter saying *Baptism, which corresponds to this, now saves you, not as a removal of dirt from the body through the resurrection of Jesus Christ, who has gone into heaven and is at the right hand of God, with angels, authorities, and powers having been subjected to him"*.[299] The writer of Hebrews gives another example from chapter twelve verses twenty two through twenty-four, *"but you have come to Mount Zion and to the city of the living God, the heavenly Jerusalem, and to innumerable angels in festal gathering, and to the assembly of the firstborn who are enrolled in heaven, and to God, the judge of all, and to the spirits of the righteous made perfect, and to Jesus, the mediator of a new covenant, and to the sprinkled blood that speaks a better word than the blood of Abel"*. In this passage there are several things mentioned, and each as distinct objects: angels, the assembly of the

---

[299] 1Peter 3:21-22

firstborn, the spirits of the righteous, the blood, and the blood of Abel, along with Jesus and God. Therefore, just as Jesus is not an angel, the blood of Abel or the spirit of the righteous, he as well is not God.

Two more things I want to bring to the reader's attention; God is the judge of all, and Jesus is the mediator. Earlier in the chapter about Jesus being a man I quoted a verse that says this exact thing[300], that he is with God as a mediator, which clarifies there is one God. If anyone can come to a conclusion contrary to this after considering these undeniable proofs, I doubt anything would have an effect on what they accept as true.

---

[300] 1 Timothy 2:5

12 Revelation

Revelation is said by some to suggest Jesus, described as the lamb, is the eternal Creator. But I reject that deceptive and dishonest exegesis of the book. One main reason for this, as I have already mentioned in a previous chapter, we are told in the very beginning that the Revelation was given by God to Jesus, as it says, *"The revelation of Jesus Christ, which God gave him to show to his servants the things that must soon take place. He made it known by sending his angel to his servant John"*[301].

So, delving into the letter I am going to post some rather lengthy passages because I think context is important to back one's doctrinal stance from scripture.

The first of these begins with verse one of chapter four which then carries over and finishes in the final verse of chapter five. As I go through these verses, I want to bring out some important things that John saw in his vision, which will be seen in footnotes mostly because of the length of the passage.

It begins, *"After this I looked, and behold, a door standing open in heaven! And the first voice, which I had heard speaking to me like a trumpet, said,*

---

[301] Revelation 1:1

"Come up here, and I will show you what must take place after this." At once I was in the Spirit, and behold, a throne stood in heaven, with one seated on the throne.[302] *And he who sat there had the appearance of jasper and carnelian, and around the throne was a rainbow that had the appearance of an emerald. Around the throne were twenty-four thrones, and seated on the thrones were twenty-four elders, clothed in white garments, with golden crowns on their heads. From the throne came flashes of lightning, and rumblings and peals of thunder, and before the throne were burning seven torches of fire, which are the seven spirits of God*[303]*, and before the throne there was as it were a sea of glass, like crystal. And around the throne, on each side of the throne, are four living creatures, full of eyes in front and behind: the first living creature like a lion, the second living creature like an ox, the third living creature with the face of a man, and the fourth living creature like an eagle in flight. And the four living creatures, each of them with six wings, are full of eyes all around and within, and day and night they never cease to say, "Holy, holy, holy, is the Lord God*

---

[302] This is important to recognize, there is only one seated on this throne whom he next says had the appearance of…

[303] John makes mention of this in chapter one verse four, *"Grace to you and peace from him who is and who was and who is to come, and from the seven spirits who are before his throne"* which then follows with *"and from Jesus Christ the faithful witness"*. I would think this to be another evidence that would clear up any questions about this issue, but over fifteen hundred years later people still argue against this simple truth that Jesus is not the one sitting on the throne

Almighty, who was and is and is to come!" And whenever the living creatures give glory and honor and thanks to him who is seated on the throne, who lives forever and ever, the twenty-four elders fall down before him who is seated on the throne and worship him who lives forever and ever. They cast their crowns before the throne, saying, "Worthy are you, our Lord and God, to receive glory and honor and power, for you created all things, and by your will they existed and were created. Then I saw in the right hand of him who was seated on the throne a scroll written within and on the back, sealed with seven seals.[304] And I saw a strong angel proclaiming with a loud voice, "Who is worthy to open the scroll and break its seals?" And no one in heaven or on earth or under the earth was able to open the scroll or to look into it, and I began to weep loudly because no one was found worthy to open the scroll or to look into it. And one of the elders said to me, "Weep no more; behold, the Lion of the tribe of Judah, the Root of David, has conquered, so that he can open the scroll and its seven seals." And between the throne and the four living creatures and among the elders I saw a Lamb standing, as though it had been slain, with seven horns and with seven eyes, which are the seven spirits of God sent out into all the earth. And he went and took the scroll from the right hand of

---

[304] The one who is seated on the throne is none other than the Lord God. It is important to remember John writes there was *"one seated on the throne"*, not two or three. He does though mention twenty-four thrones around the Lord Gods

him who was seated on the throne.[305] *And when he had taken the scroll, the four living creatures and the twenty-four elders fell down before the Lamb, each holding a harp, and golden bowls full of incense, which are the prayers of the saints. And they sang a new song, saying, "Worthy are you to take the scroll and to open its seals, for you were slain, and by your blood you ransomed people for God from every tribe and language and people and nation, and you have made them a kingdom and priests to our God, and they shall reign on the earth."*[306] *Then I looked, and I heard around the throne and the living creatures and the elders the voice of many angels, numbering myriads of myriads and thousands of thousands, saying with a loud voice, "Worthy is the Lamb who was slain, to receive power and wealth and wisdom and might and honor and glory and blessing!" And I heard every creature in heaven and on earth and under the earth and in the sea, and all that is in them, saying, "To him who sits on the throne and to the Lamb be blessing and honor and glory and might forever and ever!" And the four living creatures said, "Amen!" and the elders fell down and worshiped.*

Besides the fact that Jesus was said to have been given this by God as well as the one on the throne

---

[305] Of course, the Lamb is a reference to Jesus the Messiah. The interesting thing is that he takes the scroll from *him who was seated on the throne*, who earlier the apostle explained was the Lord God. So, we have Jesus, the lamb, taking the scroll from the Lord God

[306] This is another confirmation that they did not view the lamb, i.e. Jesus, as God

being his God as John pens in chapter one verses four through six.

The next passage comes from chapter seven beginning with verse nine and ending with verse seventeen. John begins in verse nine with, *"After this I looked, and behold, a great multitude that no one could number, from every nation, from all tribes and peoples and languages, standing before the throne and before the Lamb, clothed in white robes, with palm branches in their hands, and crying out with a loud voice, "Salvation belongs to our God who sits on the throne, and to the Lamb!" And all the angels were standing around the throne and around the elders and the four living creatures, and they fell on their faces before the throne and worshiped God, saying, "Amen! Blessing and glory and wisdom and thanksgiving and honor and power and might be to our God forever and ever! Amen." Then one of the elders addressed me, saying, "Who are these, clothed in white robes, and from where have they come?" I said to him, "Sir, you know." And he said to me, "These are the ones coming out of the great tribulation. They have washed their robes and made them white in the blood of the Lamb.* "Therefore they are before the throne of God, and serve him day and night in His temple; and He who sits on the throne will shelter them with His presence. They shall hunger no more, neither thirst anymore; the sun shall not strike them, nor any scorching heat. For the Lamb in the midst of the throne will be their *shepherd, and he will guide them to springs of living water, and God will wipe away every tear from their eyes".*

The apostle leaves no doubts as to who God is not in this passage.

This can first be seen in his statement *"before the throne and before the Lamb"*. It has already been shown that the throne is speaking of *the Lord God Almighty's* throne, which John verifies in verse ten saying, *"Salvation belongs to our God who sits on the throne, and to the Lamb"*. Notice it says, *"salvation belongs to our God who sits on the throne and"* indicating that he is about to introduce a person apart from the one *who sits on the throne*. This person is the Lamb, of whom we are told by John the Baptist is Je-sus, as he proclaims when he sees him, *"behold the lamb of God"*. This clearly shows that the Lamb is not sitting on the throne.

More evidence to prove this fact can be found in chapter one verses four through six, in which Jesus is said to *"make us a kingdom, priests to his God and Father"*. We also find in this passage John writes that those before God's throne say, *"blessing and glory and wisdom and thanksgiving and honor and power and might be to our God forever and ever"*. These beings before His throne say this same thing in chapter five, *"you have made them a kingdom and priests to our God, and they shall reign on the earth"*[307].

---

[307] Revelation 5:10

Furthermore, as has already been said, the apostle writes of Jesus, that it is before his God that he made us a kingdom and priests just as they proclaim here. This is found in chapter twenty verses four and six, *"Then I saw thrones, and seated on them were those to whom the authority to judge was committed. Also I saw the souls of those who had been beheaded for the testimony of Jesus and for the word of God, and those who had not worshiped the beast or its image and had not received its mark on their foreheads or their hands. They came to life and reigned with Christ for a thousand years... Blessed and holy is the one who shares in the first resurrection! Over such the second death has no power, but they will be priests of God and of Christ, and they will reign with him for a thousand years.* There is also this verse that speaks of this kingdom *"heard a loud voice in heaven, saying, "Now the salvation and the power and the kingdom of our God and the authority of His Christ have come..."*[308].

It should be obvious from what John has written, that God is a single person, of whom everyone is subject to, including the messiah.

To end this section, I will give the reader this verse to read. *"Then I saw another sign in heaven, great and amazing, seven angels with seven plagues, which are the last, for with them the wrath of God is finished. And I saw what appeared to be a sea of glass mingled with fire-and also those who had*

---

[308] Revelation 12:10

conquered the beast and its image and the number of its name, standing beside the sea of glass with harps of God in their hands. And they sing the song of Moses, the servant of God, and the song of the Lamb, saying, "Great and amazing are your deeds, O Lord God the Almighty! Just and true are your ways, O King of the nations! Who will not fear, O Lord, and glorify your name? For you alone are holy. All nations will come and worship you, for your righteous acts have been revealed"—Revelation 15:1-4

Conclusion

In ending I am going to start with this quote concerning the person of God: *"What is personality? The ability to have emotion, will, to express oneself. Rocks cannot speak. Cats cannot think of themselves over against others, and, say, work for the common good of "cat kind." Hence, we are saying that there is one eternal, infinite being of God, shared fully and completely by three persons, Father, Son and Spirit. One **what**, three **who's**"*.[309]

This writer supports the notion that YHWH is a three-person singular being, and accepts the idea that this three headed being, *who's* that are a *what*[310], can speak as an *I, me, mine* or *he, his, him* and still be three individuals. I have yet to hear a sensible explanation according to any known language exactly how this can be validated. The only response I have heard is "it's a mystery" which I concur with seeing it is not found in scripture, thus, is as far from the truth as it could possibly be.

I want to offer a challenging thought to consider, despite the fact that it may be considered foolish by

---

[309] *A Brief Definition of the Trinity*, James White

[310] If he were honest, he would have to say his infinite being is one *it* and three *who's*. I would also like to suggest that they refer to God as a *what* because that is what everyone says after it is attempted to be explained

some, though, I must say, no more foolish than one *what* and three *who's*.

It has to be taken into consideration when attempting to explain how these three persons are one co-equal personal being. These facts have to be explained: we have in scripture no mention of *God the son* or *God the spirit*, but it does insistently say *God the Father*. However, we do see scripture say *the son of God* and *the spirit of God*. So, scripture decisively shows these two persons/beings belong to God, that is, are of God, which I suppose could make Him a *what*. But a peculiar thing you never see is the statement, *Father of God*. Bearing in mind the claim that God is a coequal multi-personal being, I find it unusual that all three are not equally said to be *…of God* or referred to as *God the…* There cannot be co-equality when there is an absence of uniformity in how each character is defined or labeled.

Considering all of the indisputable evidence presented, to insist on a multi-person God corrupts the authenticity of God's word to man, plunges those who are adherents into the practice of idol worship and destroys the glory of what Jesus achieved. We, as students of scripture, should be honest in our studies and not let ourselves to be blinded by the subjectivity of a long-held tradition hinder us in seeking to understand God and His scriptures. The answer to this debate is simple, God is our Father, and everything else belongs to Him.

I leave this quote to think over:

"the doctrine of the Trinity is...subversive of the first great truth of the Jewish religion, it demanded ten-fold weight of evidence to set the old doctrine aside and make room for the introduction of the new. The new doctrine, therefore, would have been proclaimed in a style suited to its dignity — preached in the streets, and shouted from the house tops — argued in the school, and thundered forth in the synagogue, established by miracles for the satisfaction of the multitude, and demonstrated with power for the conviction of the learned. An object so weighty would not have been based on an epithet or exclamation, nor left to pendulant by the spider-thread of an inference. The use of the Greek article, or Hebrew plural, the precise meaning of an obscure word, or ambiguous phrase, or the admission or rejection of a text stamped with the brand of interpolation, would have had little influence in a question of such magnitude. That which was intended to illuminate the world, would not, in contradiction to a declaration of the Saviour, have been hid "under a bushel," but presented to us in a volume of light, and made to shine upon us like the sun in his brightness, that all might see and understand".[311]

> *Jesus_answered_him, "It is written, "'You shall worship the Lord your God, and him only shall you serve.'—Luke 4:8*

---

[311] *The Doctrine of The Trinity, Founded Neither on Scripture, Nor on Reason and Common Sense, But on Tradition and The Infallible Church* – Essay by William H. Drummond

Scripture Index

All scripture is quoted from the English Standard version unless otherwise noted

One God

Deuteronomy- (6:4) – Mark (10:21) – Luke (1:32) –John (5:43-34) (12:49-50) (14:10) (17:1-2, 3) – Acts (2:36) (4:24-32) – 1Corinthians(8:4-6) (15:28) – Ephesians (4:4-6) – 1Timothy- (1:1-2, 17) (2:5) – James (1:17) (2:19) – Jude (1:25) – Revelation (21:3)

God Is Ours and Jesus's Father

Exodus (33:19) – Judges (3:9) – Psalms (119:76) – Nehemiah (9:27) – Isaiah (48:9-11) – Matthew (1:21, 22) (6:9) (7:21) (11:25-26) (28:18) – Mark (9:7) – Luke (1:31-35) (6:35-36) (10:21) – John (1:18) (3:16) (4:25) (7:31) (8:29, 58) (10:13) (12:43, 50) (14:20) (17:1, 3, 22, 23) (20:17-18, 21, 25) – Acts (4:24-30) – Romans (1:1-10) (2:7) (5:10) (15:5-7) (16:27) – 1Corinthians (1:1-9) – 2Corinthians (1:1-4) (11:31) – Galatians (1:1-5) – Ephesians (1:1-6) (4:14-21) (5:20) (6:23) – Philippians(1:1-11)(2:9-

11) (4:19-20) – Colossians (1:1-3, 3-4) – 1Thessalonians (1:1-10) (2:13-17) (3:11-13) – 2Thessalonians (1:1-12) (2:16-17) – 1Timothy (1:1-2) (2:5) – 2 Timothy (1:1-2) – Titus (1:1-4) – Philemon (1:3-6) – James (1:27) – 1 Peter (1:2-5, 21) (4:11) – 2 Peter (1:17) – 1John (1:3) (2:1-2) (3:21-23) (4:9-16) (5:20) – 2John (1:3-4) – Jude (1:1) – Revelation (1:1-6, 8) (5:9-10)

God referred to as Father

-Old Testament-

Malachi (2:10)

-Gospels, someone other than Jesus calling God Father-

John (1:14) (1:18) (3:35) (5:18) (8:27) (8:41) (13:1) (13:3) (14:8)

-Gospels, Jesus calling God Father-

Matthew (5:16) (5:45) (5:48) (6:1) (6:4) (6:6) (6:8) (6:9) (6:14) (6:15) (6:18) (6:26) (6:32) (7:11) (7:21) (10:20) (10:29) (10:32) (10:33) (11:25) (12:50)(13:43) (15:13) (16:17) (16:27) (18:10) (18:14) (18:19) 18:35, 20:23, 23:9, 26:29, 26:53 - Mark 8:38, 11:25, - Luke 2:49, 6:36, 9:26, 10:21-22, 11:2, 11:13, 12:30, 12:32, 22:29, 22:42, 23:34, 23:46, 24:49 - John 2:16, 4:21, 4:23, 5:17, 5:19, 5:20, 5:21, 5:22, 5:23, 5:26, 5:27, 5:43, 5:45, 6:27, 6:32, 6:37, 6:40, 6:44, 6:45, 6:46, 6:57, 6:65, 8:16, 8:18, 8:19, 8:28, 8:38, 8:42, 8:49, 8:54, 10:15,

10:17, 10:18, 10:25, 10:29, 10:30, 10:32, 10:36, 10:37, 10:38, 12:26, 12:27, 12:28, 12:49, 12:50, 14:2, 14:6-13, 14:16, 14:20, 14:21, 14:23, 14:24, 14:26, 14:28, 14:31, 15:1, 15:8-10, 15:15-16, 15:23-24, 15:26, 16:3, 16:10, 16:15, 16:15, 16:17, 16:23, 16:25, 16:26-28, 16:32, 17:1, 17:5, 17:11, 17:21, 17:24-25, 18:11, 18:13, 20:17, 20:21

-Epistles-

Acts 1:4, 1:7, 2:33 – Romans 1:7, 6:4, 8:15, 15:6 – 1Corinthians 1:3, 8:6, 15:24 – 2Corinthians 1:2-3, 11:31 – Galatians 1:1, 1:3, 11:31 – Ephesians 1:2-3, 1:17, 2:18, 3:14, 4:6, 5:20, 6:23 – Philippians 1:2, 2:11, 4:20 – Colossians 1:2-3, 1:12, 3:17 – 1Thessalonians 1:1, 1:3, 3:11, 3:13 – 2Thessalonians 1:1-2, 2:16 – 1Timothy 1:2 – 2Timothy 1:2 – Titus 1:4 – Philemon 1:3 – Hebrews 12:9 – James 1:17, 1:27, 3:9 – 1Peter 1:2-3, 1:17 – 2Peter 1:17 – 1John 1:2-3, 2:1, 2:13, 2:15-16, 2:22 -24, 3:1, 4:14, 5:1 – 2John 1:3-4, 1:9 – Jude 1:1 – Revelation 1:6, 2:27, 3:5, 3:21, 14:1

-Jesus called son-

Matthew 1:1, 2:15, 3:17, 4:3, 4:6, 8:29, 9:6, 9:27, 10:28, 11:19, 11:27, 12:23, 12:32, 12:40, 13:37, 13:41, 13:55, 14:33, 15:22, 16:13, 16:16, 16:27, 16:28, 17:5, 17:9, 17:13, 17:15, 17:22, 18:11, 19:28, 20:18, 20:28, 20:30, 21:9, 21:15, 22:42, 22:45, 24:27, 24:30, 24:27, 24:44, 25:13, 25:31, 26:2, 26:24, 26:45, 26:63-64, 27:40, 27:43, 27:54,

28:19 – Luke 1:31-32, 1:35, 3:22, 3:38, 4:3, 4:9, 5:24, 6:5, 6:22, 7:34, 8:28, 9:22, 9:26, 9:35, 9:44, 9:56, 9:58, 10:22, 11:30, 12:8, 12:10, 12:40, 17:22, 17:24, 17:26, 17:30, 18:8, 18:31, 18:38, 19:10, 10:40, 20:44, 21:27, 21:36, 22:22, 22:48, 22:69, 22:70, 24:7 – John 1:18, 1:34, 1:49, 1:51, 3:13, 3:14, 3:16, 3:17, 3:18, 3:35, 3:36, 5:19, 5:20, 5:21, 5:22, 5:23, 5:25, 5:26, 5:27, 6:27, 6:40, 6:53, 6:62, 6:69, 8:28, 8:35, 8:36, 9:35, 10:36, 11:4, 11:27, 12:22, 12:34, 13:31, 14:13, 17:1, 19:7, 20:31 – Acts 3:13, 3:26, 7:56, 8:37, 9:20, 13:33 – Romans 1:3, 1:4, 1:9, 5:10, 8:3, 8:29, 8:32 – 1 Corinthians 1:9, 15:28 – 2 Corinthians 1:19 – Galatians 1:16, 2:20, 4:4, 4:6 – Ephesians 4:23 – Colossians 1:10 – 1 Thessalonians 1:10 – Hebrews 1:2, 1:5, 1:8, 3:6, 4:14, 5:5, 5:8, 6:6, 7:3, 7:28, 10:29, 11:17 – 2 Peter 1:17 – 1John 1:3, 1:7, 2:22, 2:23, 2:24, 3:8, 3:23, 4:9, 4:10, 4:14, 4:15, 5:5, 5:9, 5:10, 5:11, 5:12, 5:13, 5:20 – 2 John 1:3, 1:9 – Revelation 1:13, 2:18, 14:14, 21:7

Jesus Teaches How to Pray

Isaiah 63:8 –Matthew 15) (23:9) (26:39, 42) – Mark (14:35-36) – Luke (6:12) – John (8:41-42) (8:54) (11:41-42) (17:1, 9) (20:17)

Jesus Raised from the Dead

Deuteronomy (18:18) – 1 Chronicles (29:18, 2) Chronicles (20:6) – Psalms (40:7-10) – Micah (5:2) – Matthew (16:16) (17:5) (28:19-20) – Mark (1:11) – Luke 3:22) (4:14, 18-19) – John 3:16) (4:25) (8:29) (14:31) (15:27) (17:1, 24) – Acts (1:7-8) (2:32) (3:13-15, 22-26) (4:18-19) (5:30-31) (10:34-42) (13:23, 26-39) – Romans (1:4) (4:24-25) (8:11) (8:32-34) (15:13) – 1 Corinthians (1:8) (6:11, 14) (15:13) – Galatians (1:1) – Ephesians (1:16-20, 20-23) – Philippians (4:19) – Colossians (1:15-18) (2:12) – 1 Thessalonians (1:9b-10) (4:14) – 1 Timothy 2:4 – Titus (3:4-7) – Hebrews (13:20-21) – 1 Peter (1:3) (20-21)

Jesus Given Authority

Matthew – (65) (28:18)Mark(3:35) (13:2) – Luke (10:21-23) (20:20-26) (23:2) – John (1:18) (3:32-36) (4:21, 23-24, 25-26, 34) (5:26-27) (6:68, 40) (7:16-18, 26, 28-29, 47-48) (8:16, 25, 28-29, 47) (12:49-50) (13:3-4) (14:10, 24) (17:1-2, 11-12, 14, 18, 24) (20:23) – Acts (1:7) (2:22) (10:38, 42) – 1Corinthians (15:24, 25-28) – Ephesians (1:7-10, 16-23) – Philippians (2:9-11) – 2 Timothy (4:1, 8) – Revelation (2:26-27, 12:10, 20:6, 14)

Through or In Jesus

Exodus (19:5-6) – Isaiah (66:21-22) – Matthew (1:21) (10:20-21) – Luke (11:25) (24:46) – John

(3:16, 2) (8:31-32)(14:17, 24, 31)(17:17) – Acts (2:31, 32, 36) (5:30-31) – Romans (3:21-25) (5:1-2, 10-11, 21) (8:34) (15:33) (16:25-27) – 1Corinthians (1:3, 8:4-6, 15:24, 57) (16:25-27) – 2Corinthians (5:18-19, 11:31) – Ephesians (1:4-6, 16-21) (2:4-10, 2-3) (3:8-19) – Philippians (4-7) – Colossians (1:15-17, 19-18) (3:1, 16-17) – 1Thessalonians (1:2, 3) (2:12) (5:9-10) – 2Thessalonians (2:13-14) – Titus (3:4-7) – Hebrew (1:1-2) (13:20-21) – 1Peter (2:5) (4:10-11) (5:10-11) – 1John (5:20)

Jesus Is a Man

1Chronicles (22:10) – Daniel (7:13-14) – Matthew (8:9) (10:33, 41) (11:47-50) (26:63) (28:18) – John Acts (10:38) – Romans (15:15, 17, 19) – 1Corinthians (10:13) (15:21-23, 42-49) – 1Timothy (2:5) – Hebrews (4:15)

Jesus Belongs to God

1Corinthians (1:3) (3:21-23) (11:3) (15:24, 28) – Hebrews (10:7)

Jesus Is with God

Mark (16:19) – Acts (2:33) (5:31) (7:55) (8:34) (17:30-31) – Ephesians (1:17, 19-20) – Philippians (2:9) – Colossians (3:1) – 1Timothy (5:21) (6:13) – 2Timothy (2:5) (4:1-2) – 1Peter (3:21-22)

Revelation

(1:1) (1:4-6) (4:1-5:14) (12:10) (7:9-17) (20:4-6)

www.ingramcontent.com/pod-product-compliance
Lightning Source LLC
Chambersburg PA
CBHW070849050426
42453CB00012B/2096